On the Boards

On the Boards

Drawings by Nineteenth-Century Boston Architects

James F. O'Gorman

UNIVERSITY OF PENNSYLVANIA PRESS *upp*

PHILADELPHIA   1989

On the occasion of the exhibition
"ON THE BOARDS: DRAWINGS BY
NINETEENTH-CENTURY BOSTON
ARCHITECTS"
  Wellesley College Museum, Wellesley, Massachusetts
  April 15–June 11, 1989

This exhibition was organized and the catalogue prepared with
the assistance of a grant from the National Endowment for the
Arts. The catalogue is published with the assistance of the
Graham Foundation for Advanced Studies in the Fine Arts.

Photo credit: Cat. 70a–c and Plate 14,
Richard Cheek, Belmont, Massachusetts.

Library of Congress Cataloging-in-Publication Data

O'Gorman, James F.
  On the boards: drawings by nineteenth-century Boston
architects / James F. O'Gorman.
     p.   cm.
  Catalogue of an exhibition held at Wellesley College Museum.
  Includes index.
  ISBN 0-8122-8170-5. ISBN 0-8122-1287-8 (pbk.)
  1. Architectural drawing—19th century—Massachusetts—
Boston—Exhibitions. I. Wellesley College. Museum.
II. Title.
NA2706.U6036 1989
720'.22'2—dc19   88-27850
                                           CIP

*To the Boston Architectural Center
in its centennial year, 1889–1989*

Contents

Lenders to the Exhibition

Drawings and Archives, Avery Architectural and Fine Arts Library, Columbia University in the City of New York

Memorial Library, Boston Architectural Center

Boston Athenaeum

The Gibbons Preston Fine Arts Department, The Boston Public Library; Courtesy of the Trustees of the Boston Public Library

Cape Ann Historical Association, Gloucester, Massachusetts

Harvard University Archives

Harvard University Planning Office

Department of Printing and Graphic Arts, Houghton Library, Harvard University

Prints and Photographs Division, Library of Congress

The M.I.T. Museum

The National Archives, Washington, D.C.

I. N. Phelps Stokes Collection; The Miriam and Ira D. Wallach Division of Art, Prints, and Photographs; The New York Public Library; Astor, Lenox and Tilden Foundations

Department of Art and Architecture, Northeastern University

Private Collection

Division of Archives and History, City Hall,
    Providence, Rhode Island

Milton and Homai Schmidt

Earle G. Shettleworth, Jr.

Society for the Preservation of New England
    Antiquities, Boston, Massachusetts

Wellesley College Archives

Paul White

Acknowledgments

ALTHOUGH THE SELECTION, annotation, and introduction of the architectural drawings in the following catalogue were the labor of one individual, I have depended heavily upon the cooperation and contributions of many librarians, scholars, curators, collectors, teachers, and friends who have given generously of their time and their knowledge:

Ellie Reichlin of the Society for the Preservation of New England Antiquities; *Roberta Waddell* of the New York Public Library; *Dr. and Mrs. Milton Schmidt; Janet Parks* and *Herbert Mitchell* of the Avery Library, Columbia University; *Wheaton Holden; Paul White; Mr. and Mrs. William B. Osgood; Earle G. Shettleworth, Jr.,* of the Maine Historic Preservation Commission; *Margaret Henderson Floyd* of Tufts University; *Christopher P. Monkhouse* of the Museum of Art, Rhode Island School of Design; *Susan Danly; Douglass Shand Tucci; Jean A. Follett; Sally Pierce* and *Harry Katz* of the Print Room, Boston Athenaeum; *Martha Oaks* of the Cape Ann Historical Association; *Robin McElheny* of Harvard University Archives; *Eleanor Garvey* of the Houghton Library, Harvard University; *C. Ford Peatross* of the Prints and Photographs Division, Library of Congress; *Wilma Slaight* of the Wellesley College Archives; *Cervin Robinson; John Zukowsky* of the Burnham Library, Chicago Art Institute; *Jack Quinan* of the State University of New York at Buffalo; *Janice H. Chadbourne* of the Fine Arts Department, Boston Public Library; *Michael Yates* of the M.I.T. Museum; *Susan Lewis* of the Boston Architectural Center; *Georgia Barnhill* of the American Antiquarian Society; *Greer Hardwicke* of the Brookline Historical Commission; *Susan Maycock* of the Cambridge Historical Commission; *Robert Drake* of the Harvard University Planning Office; *Philip Bergen* of the Bostonian Society; *Ross Urquhart* of the Massachusetts Historical Society; *Anne Kinnear* of the Hull Historical Commission; *Carol B. Pace* of the Division of Archives and History, City Hall, Providence, Rhode Island; and *Catherine H. Allen* of the Grace Slack McNeil Program at Wellesley College.

For their assistance in attending to all details of mounting the exhibition at the Wellesley College Museum and coordinating this publication, I would like to thank *Susan M. Taylor*, Director; *Lucy Flint-Gohlke*, Assistant Director; *Polly Giragosian*, Curatorial Assistant; and *Nancy Swallow*, Registrar. Special thanks are due to *Jennifer Dowd Mason*, former Registrar, who was responsible for handling logistical aspects of the project in its earliest stages.

J.F. O'G.
1 June 1988

Preface

The Wellesley College Museum is pleased to present the exhibition *On the Boards: Drawings by Nineteenth-Century Boston Architects*, curated by James O'Gorman, Grace Slack McNeil Professor of American Art at Wellesley College. The first such synthesis of this material, the exhibition examines the evolving role of the architectural drawing in the development of the profession in the nineteenth century. Professor O'Gorman has observed that while the history of architecture is based primarily on the evidence of built monuments, there is a rich but too infrequently remarked lode of information about the subject preserved in architects' drawings for unbuilt as well as realized projects. For this reason, well-known drawings by well-known architects, such as the 1795 plan and elevation by Bulfinch of the Massachusetts State House or the 1885 sketch from H. H. Richardson's office of the Marshall Field store in Chicago, share the walls with unknown or little-known works by unknown or little-known designers, including Luther Briggs's 1856 project for a college in Liberia or Edwin Tobey's design for the Hull Yacht Club.

The drawings for this exhibition were selected on the basis of typology, historical importance, and visual appeal. The full range of architectural graphics is represented, from the initial sketch to the contract document. The exhibition shows the ways in which the historical development of architectural graphics—from the plan-and-upright orthographics of the late eighteenth and early nineteenth centuries to the richly optical presentation perspectives of the late nineteenth and early twentieth centuries—parallels the stylistic evolution of Boston architecture and the architectural profession during the same period. The place of these graphics in the history of architecture and the architectural profession in nineteenth-century Boston are examined, and detailed catalogue information is provided for each object.

Exhibitions that serve as teaching instruments while providing visual enrichment for students and for the public have held an important place in the study of art at Wellesley since the opening of the Museum in 1889. Included in the present exhibition is an unsigned preliminary drawing of the Farnsworth Art Museum, the College's museum until 1958. Designed by Boston architects Arthur Rotch and George Thomas Tilden, the building provided exhibition space as well as facilities for the teaching and making of art. The opening of Farnsworth allowed the arts to flourish at Wellesley and marked the beginning of one hundred years of sustained museum activity. Interest in architecture is a tradition at Wellesley that was established as early as 1899, when the Museum devoted its first major loan exhibition to architectural drawings that included "original sketches in pencil and in colors" (*Wellesley Magazine*, April 1900). Among the drawings included in the exhibition was " . . . a very attractive watercolor, all in greys and olives of the church at Cohasset" by Bertram Grosvenor Goodhue (1869–1924), an architect who is featured in the present catalogue and accompanying exhibition—almost a century later.

On the Boards reflects an integral aspect of the Museum's programming, one which demonstrates the institution's dual commitment to education and visual enrichment. As part of its mission, the Museum has consistently supported the work of members of the art department in new areas of research. We are pleased to continue that tradition with this exhibition. As we begin the celebration of the first hundred years of the Museum at Wellesley, it is gratifying to inaugurate the 1989 exhibition schedule with a project so representative of the Museum's goals and past achievements.

The Museum would like to thank the University of Pennsylvania Press, particularly Jo Mugnolo, Arthur Evans, and Ruth Veleta, for their scrupulous attention to this catalogue. It has been a great pleasure to work with them.

We also wish to acknowledge several funding sources that have made the exhibition and catalogue possible. To the National Endowment for the Arts, we extend our gratitude—as we have so many times in the past—for its support. The catalogue is published with the assistance of the Graham Foundation for Advanced Studies in the Fine Arts, dedicated to furthering the study of art and architecture through its generous grants. We also thank the Grace Slack McNeil Program in American Art for support provided for the exhibition. In the fourteen years of its existence, the program has greatly enriched the offerings at Wellesley, sponsoring several important exhibitions and catalogues, as well as lectures and symposia for the College and the Boston area.

Finally, our gratitude and appreciation are extended to James O'Gorman, curator of this presentation. His commitment to and enthusiasm for the project have ensured that *On the Boards* represents a significant contribution to a growing body of work devoted to the examination of architectural drawings.

SUSAN M. TAYLOR
Director
Wellesley College Museum

Abbreviations

AABN	*The American Architect and Building News*
JSAH	*Journal of the Society of Architectural Historians*
MEA	Adolf Placzek, ed., *The Macmillan Encyclopedia of Architects*, New York, 1982

Prolegomenon

DRAWINGS OUGHT PROPERLY to be the central focus of architectural history. While the finished building is often the product of economic and other compromises, and at its best represents a compatible collaborative effort for which the designer is only partly responsible, what the architect has "on the boards," his drawings for work in progress, represents the purest expression of his architectural ideas and ideals. That architectural drawings are created as vehicles toward building should not be forgotten, but it is possible to learn more about the intention of a designer by studying his graphic remains than by visiting his built legacy.[1] Or, perhaps a more desirably balanced approach, full understanding is to be approximated by checking the one against the other. Be that as it may, no history of American building can approximate completeness until the graphic remains of the collective design process have been studied in some detail. If this modest selection of largely unpublished work from one century in one urban center (which joins recent surveys of other areas[2]) quickens developing interest in the preservation and study of this archival material, it will have well served its purpose.

This small gathering of drawings by nineteenth-century Boston architects for both local and distant buildings is the result of grazing through thousands of sheets, largely during the fall of 1987. Inclusion was based upon a number of factors: the historical significance of a drawing either intrinsically or as representative of a type, the desire to present as broad a spectrum of graphic types as possible, the wish to include the work of little known as well as familiar architects, and—since this is first of all the catalogue of a museum exhibition—a drawing's visual appeal. Selection was adversely affected by the accidents of preservation, conservation, or availability. Despite omissions that are probably more glaring to the author than anyone else, this seems—given the restricted number of drawings—a reasonably representative introduction to the graphic remains of local architects from Charles Bulfinch to Ralph Adams Cram.[3]

This is the catalogue of an exhibition of typical Boston architectural graphics of the last century. Although this brief prolegomenon provides something of a broad historical overview, it is not a history of Boston architecture or architectural design of the last century illustrated by drawings,[4] nor is it a history of architectural drawing. As the architect's phrase "on the boards" indicates work in progress, so this catalogue is intended to initiate ongoing discussion. It is conceived as a "sampler": an introduction to draftsmen, their paper products, and the surviving heritage of architectural drawings associated with the profession in nineteenth-century Boston. Discussions of drawings have often used them as windows through which to look at the buildings they present. Architectural graphics do not exist as ends in themselves, and any meaningful discussion must include, where possible, observations about the design and construction of the buildings they prescribe. The main concern here, however, is for drawings as drawings, and for their evolving characteristics.

Architectural drawings vary in character according to a variety of factors, among them the skill of the draftsman and the period in which the drawing is made.[5] Construction at the end of the twentieth century requires a vast number of sheets (or "contract documents") because of our myriad design options, the complexity of structural and mechanical components, and the litigious climate of the times. In the eighteenth and early nineteenth centuries, conditions were otherwise, and the drawings that have survived from that era are consequently distinctly different from current production. They are frequently complete with plan(s) and elevation(s). Architectural drawings also vary in appearance depending upon the reasons for which they were made.[6] Their place within the spectrum of architectural graphics, from initial sketch (Cat. 51) to finished working drawing (Cat. 78a–c), will affect their look. Whether a drawing is for personal or intramural use (Cat. 54) or for public or promotional exhibition or publication (Cat. 39) will mark a sheet; whether it is drawn by a principal or his assistant: these and other factors account for the broad range of graphic types produced in formulating a building design. All are necessary to the process, and all are proper to the study of architectural drawing. As many types as possible are included in this catalogue.

Although this is the catalogue of a museum exhibition, the characteristics of architects' drawings which distinguish them from those of artists have been recognized. No single drawing is sufficient to explain a building. The single image, while not meaning*less*, is not meaning*ful* either. Only multiple graphics reveal the various aspects of a design, no matter how simple the building: view(s), plan(s), elevation(s), sections(s), and detail(s). Many individual architectural drawings have *artistic* value, but only a series of drawings has *architectural* value. For this reason, in this catalogue when possible, several sheets from a set of drawings have been included.

The nineteenth century witnessed a marked evolution in the architectural profession in America. In the beginning, in the urban east of the United States, there were clients and builders (masons and/or housewrights). Around the turn of the nineteenth century there emerged from the ranks of builders, or developed out of the class of gentlemen-dilettantes of the eighteenth century, a third party to whom the term "architect" was gradually applied.[7] From whichever background he journeyed, however, he became, during the second quarter of the nineteenth century, a distinct entity (Fig. 1), and during the second half, that entity ceased to be individual and gradually became largely corporate. This is directly reflected in the history of architectural graphics. A practice that began with housewrights or dilettantes inking "draughts" on Whatman paper resting on baize-covered parlor tables (see Charles Willson Peale's portrait of William Buckland, 1774, at the Yale University Art Gallery) ended in offices composed of numerous, usually anonymous draftsmen housed in large rooms filled with drafting boards churning out uniform drawings on linen or tracing paper ready to be fed to the blueprinting machine (Cat. 78a–c), or with artist-renderers creating eye-catching marketing graphics (Cat. 67). In the process the architect became a school-bred designer divorced from the actual work of erecting a building. He listened to the client's needs, drew the building on paper, and supervised the builder who executed his graphic directions. And, more and more, drawings became the principal means by which he achieved his aim.

Eighteenth-century architecture in English-speaking America was inspired by Andrea Palladio in composition and was traditional in materials and technology.[8] Builders organized planar brick or boarded timber-framed walls supporting wood truss roofs according to the symmetrical and hierarchical principles of the sixteenth-century Italian master. The English Palladians repeated over and over again the lessons found in his *Quattro libri dell'architettura*

Fig. 1. W. W. Wilson on steel after an unknown artist, engraved frontispiece to Edward Shaw, *The Modern Architect: or, Every Carpenter His Own Master*, Boston: Dayton and Wentworth, 1854 (Hitchcock 1156). In the preface, Shaw (1784–1855?) tells us he spent "fifteen years in the theoretical practice and science of Architectural Drawings and Plans, both ancient and modern" after twenty years in the building trades. In this scene the "modern architect" in top hat and frock coat, with ruler and compass in hand, is distinquished from the bareheaded, shirtsleeved workers. While they work or watch, he sits at a makeshift desk, directing building operations by interpreting his graphic directions. Boston Athenaeum.

(1570) in a literature that ranged from heavy folios that caused the shelves of gentlemen's libraries to sag, to duodecimo handbooks shoved into the pockets of "mechanicks" on the job.[9] That literature also ranged from treatises on principles to gatherings of plates of details of the orders, of frontispieces, of window surrounds, of fireplace frames, and so on. By appropriating such details and applying them to the axial armature provided by Palladian theory, any designer, mechanic or dilettante, could achieve a respectable Georgian or Federal building.

Knowledgeable patrons and mechanics alike understood the system, so architectural graphics could be and were rudimentary.[10] Until just after the Revolution, the basic and often entire geometrical formulation of a client's wants took the form of a plan or plans and one or more, usually unshaded, elevations.[11] These were orthographic projections (in which the plane of the floor or wall is parallel to the plane of the paper, so that all relationships are exactly revealed) drawn to scale in ink, using a ruling pen on heavy Whatman paper or, occasionally, parchment. Dimensions may or may not be given; materials may or may not be indicated; details such as wall thickness, stairs, flues, and so forth may or may not be present. Such a drawing might be accompanied by written or spoken instructions provided by the client to the builder about budget, materials, dimensions, and performance. Since the Palladian system and traditional technology were givens, and the final product highly predictable, such instructions, whether geometric or verbal, could be simple indeed (Cat. 6). Drawings need show only the true relationships among geometrical shapes in plan (the "ichnography" in eighteenth-century terminology[12]) and elevation (the "orthography").

From Boston few eighteenth-century drawings survive,[13] but the mode of presentation carries into the early nineteenth century in the work of conservative designers such as Thomas Sumner. His competitive project of 1819 for the Suffolk County buildings on Leverett Street (Cat. 7) shows a thoroughly Palladian composition in typically eighteenth-century orthography augmented by the use of an even color wash. (The set of drawings for this project by the competition winner, Alexander Parris, is characterized by the same old-fashioned look.) Neither in style nor in graphic technique is there much to distinguish this design from a work of two generations earlier.

If knowledge of eighteenth-century building helps us understand eighteenth-century drawings, the drawings help us characterize the architectural ideals of the era. Planimetric graphics led to planar buildings composed of flat walls and pitched roofs. In Boston, as elsewhere in America, Georgian is an architecture of planes defining spaces: planes that are best viewed as they were drawn, head on so that the finite proportions will be apparent. With such an architecture we search in vain for graphics produced in America before the last quarter of the eighteenth century that are other than orthographic. Even when he sketched a series of alternate designs for a courthouse on the back of a window jamb at Gunston Hall in the 1750s, William Buckland graphically projected his ideas in two-dimensional notations.[14] There are only plans and elevations among these rough but miraculous survivors. The same approach characterizes the ideograms of other designers of this era and slightly later, such as Thomas Jefferson.[15] The graphic musings of colonial and early Federal architectural designers were essentially orthographic.

Such graphics lack, of course, representation of the three-dimensional relationships created by the use of linear perspective or any other method of simultaneously viewing two or three planes of a solid.[16] Certainly some sense of volume could be conveyed by gray wash shades and shadows overlaying an elevation, and many an eighteenth-century architectural drawing or published engraving does exhibit this device for creating an illusion of mass while preserving the true relationships of the orthographic surface. This is a distinguishing feature, for example, of Bulfinch's representation of the Massachusetts State House (Cat. 1), and of Asher Benjamin's design for a frontispiece of 1797 (Cat. 5). But this is a far cry from the perspective view of a projected building.

Linear perspective was a rediscovery of the *quattrocento*.[17] It was in common use among British architects and was discussed in many English publications during the eighteenth century. Brook Taylor and Joshua Kirby both produced treatises on the subject,[18] and these were to be found in American and, more specifically, Boston libraries of the late eighteenth and early nineteenth centuries.[19] Kirby's *Perspective of Architecture* (1761) was of special importance.

The development of the use of this volumetric method of design and presentation parallels the emergence of the distinguishable architect around 1800, and it accompanies the concomitant evolution of architecture from planar to plastic, from two-dimensional Georgian and Federal works to three-dimensional Greco-Roman buildings. For example: John Haviland's preliminary sketches for a U.S. mint for Philadelphia, 1829, evince a monumental neo-classical building through rough three-dimensional projections, unlike Buckland's orthographic studies for a mid-eighteenth-century courthouse.[20]

The story of the use of perspective graphics in the design and presentation of buildings can only be sketched in outline here, as the detailed investigation of the subject has yet to be written. It is certain that it is not a simple chronological progression from orthography to "scenography."[21] Bulfinch's rough preliminary sketch of 1814 for the interior of New South Church, Boston,[22] demonstrates his precocious ability to think in the round in the creation of a building, but the ideograms produced as part of the "initial impulse"[23] toward building by the hand of H.H. Richardson after the Civil War are charac-teristically orthographic (Cat. 51) in accordance with a graphic preference acquired in Paris. Whether a designer will employ orthographic or scenographic views for study or presentation will depend upon a number of factors including style and historical circumstance. The development that occurred around the turn of the nineteenth century appears to have been of great historical significance.

That American designers were conscious of the limitations of orthographic design becomes apparent about the time of the Revolution. There are caches of late eighteenth-century drawings, such as those by Thomas Jefferson, that contain nothing but orthographics,[24] but there are also isolated drawings from a variety of sources that are in perspective. John McComb, Jr., of New York seems to have been studying Taylor's or Kirby's *Perspective* as a student during the Revolution.[25] It is dangerous to jump to generalizations here, since only one perspective, in which forms are projected from one vanishing point and shaded for full modeling, survives among the more than five hundred extant Mc-Comb, Sr. and Jr., sheets. The evidence we have suggests that perspective was not a great deal more important to the McCombs than it was to Jefferson.

In this graphic climate, John Trumbull's two-point perspective of a Palladian villa of 1777[26] and Charles Bulfinch's sheet of 1788 depicting the Hollis Street Church in plan and perspective (Fig. 2),[27] stand out.[28] Trumbull had yet to visit England when he made his drawing; Bulfinch had recently returned from his grand tour, but each drawing suggests a familiarity with publications such as Kirby's. While Trumbull's villa design is unique among his few architectural drawings to survive, and in any event architecture was secondary to his career as a painter, Bulfinch's use of perspective in the Hollis Street drawing distinguishes him from early American architects. He employed three-dimensional illusion throughout his career, and he left a manuscript entitled "Principles of Perspective" among his graphic remains (Fig. 3).[29] This is an eclectic work, put to-

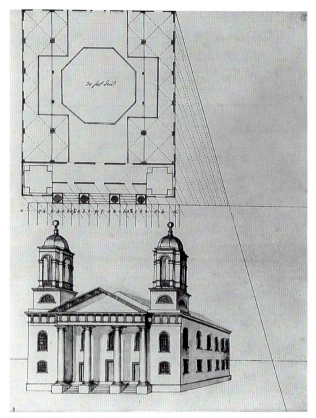

Fig. 2. Charles Bulfinch, Hollis Street Church, 1788. Plan and perspective. Bulfinch's perspective method was probably derived from Joshua Kirby's *Perspective of Architecture*, [London], 1761. Library of Congress.

gether in its present form in 1813 or after but certainly representing earlier interests, in which he assembled various methods of perspective projection learned from Kirby and others. A brief preface defines perspective as "the art of drawing, upon any surface, the representation of objects as they appear to the eye," but Bulfinch otherwise confines his remarks to *how* to draw perspectives, not *why*.

The Hollis Street Church drawing is an early example of the use of perspective, rivaled so far as is now known only by Trumbull's exercise. It repre-

sents Bulfinch's advanced geometric experience gained either at Harvard[30] or in foreign parts. In it he prescribes a Wren-inspired design in a ruled pen-and-ink drawing on paper. The projection places the front elevation of the church parallel to the picture plane (the sheet of paper) and shows the side elevation as receding to a vanishing point to the right.[31] The elevations are thus related to one another, and shade is depicted within the confines of the building itself, but there is no shadow cast upon the "ground" and no indication of ambience other than the horizon line. The inked object sits isolated on the sheet. This is very like the kind of graphic image Bulfinch would have discovered in the *Perspective of Architecture*, where Kirby reproduces both shaded and unshaded projections of buildings in copper engravings (Fig. 4). As in Bulfinch's drawing, these have their fronts parallel to the sheet and look like reproductions of models standing on smooth table tops, delimited only by an edge, or horizon.

Bulfinch's drawing of the Hollis Street Church appears to be the original draft of a presentation piece, drawn to "sell" a design. His 1802 section with interior perspective of the New North Church in Boston (Cat. 2), which shows him applying the principles he outlines in his manuscript, looks like an unfinished drawing intended for his client as well. But his rough sketch of 1814 for the interior of New South Church, Boston, appears to be a private document and shows him thinking in perspective in a way no earlier local draftsman seems to have been capable.[32] This three-dimensional graphic probing and presenting heralds the architect's later work in neo-classical style. Bulfinch would appear to have been a pacesetter in American architectural graphics, until, that is, we turn our attention to the Federal capital at Philadelphia, and the arrival in the United States of Benjamin Henry Latrobe in March of 1796.

Jefferson's amateur status as a designer of buildings is signaled in his tightly inked orthographic drawings frequently executed on controlling graph paper. Bulfinch's increasing professionalism is sig-

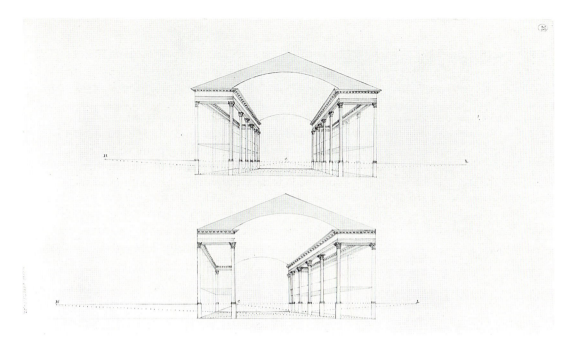

Fig. 3. Charles Bulfinch, centric and eccentric one-point perspectives of a church interior with galleries, folio 28 of his "Principles of Perspective," ca. 1813. Bulfinch left in manuscript a work in which he studied the various methods of perspective construction available to him in the early nineteenth century. Library of Congress.

Fig. 4. J. Patton on copper after Inigo Jones, Plate LX of Joshua Kirby, *The Perspective of Architecture . . . Deduced from the Principles of Dr. Brook Taylor*, [London], 1761. This illustration is taken from the copy in the Boston Athenaeum, formerly in the library of Ithiel Town, given by Asher Benjamin in 1810. Kirby's works on perspective were well studied by American draftsmen of the late eighteenth and early nineteenth century.

naled by his tentative graphic exploration of the third dimension. Latrobe arrived in America as a fully trained artist, architect, and engineer who had practiced in England. He brought with him the latest in style, technology, and graphic technique. And he revolutionized American architecture.

Latrobe's Bank of Pennsylvania of 1798 burst upon Federal Philadelphia like the dawn of a new day. That it was fronted with Grecian porticoes, the first use of this classical source in America, may have been its least important feature, although the use of Greek orders did further Latrobe's robust neo-classicism. Masonry vaults and a dome resting upon thick stone walls declared a break with flat eighteenth-century brick and wood construction, and generated a previously unknown (in America) plastic architecture that was monochromatic and monumentally scaled. All of this is announced in Latrobe's presentation drawing. It shows the exterior of the bank in its intended setting of small-scaled, pink and white, Georgian and Federal neighbors in a graphic image as revolutionary as the building it foreshadowed.[33] In one representation that combined perspective, shades and shadows, and watercolors, Latrobe made the graphic works of Jefferson, the McCombs, Trumbull, and even Bulfinch look naive.[34] In this presentation he depicted an unbuilt building as it was going to look within a specific ambience, amid the lights and shadows of a future day.

Philadelphia architects in Latrobe's wake followed his example. He generated a school of brilliant draftsmen led by William Strickland, English-born John Haviland, and T.U. Walter. Although Bulfinch's later local works seem to reflect the monumental neo-classicism introduced by Latrobe (as well as the availability of Quincy granite), his graphics remained largely unaffected by those of the immigrant. He eventually came to recognize the gap between their graphic abilities, certainly, for he wrote his wife just after replacing Latrobe as architect of the national Capitol that his predecessor's drawings were daunting: "at first view . . . , my courage almost failed me—they are beautifully executed and the design is in the boldest stile." Although he adds that closer inspection revealed that they contained "faults enough," he knew a superior draftsman when he saw one.[35] Only Bulfinch's late drawings for the Maine State House suggest some impact of Latrobe's graphic style, and that is watered down indeed.[36]

If Latrobe's accomplished draftsmanship inspired in Philadelphia a rich legacy of graphic work, Bulfinch's dry perspective constructions and usually thin, ruled-ink orthographics led to a different graphic history in Boston. In this locale, graphic development seems to have paralleled the slow evolution in building style that marked the early nineteenth century (Cat. 9). Among known surviving drawings, three-dimensional projections are very rare, and those that exist are retarded in the extreme. Alexander Parris succeeded to Bulfinch's work on the Massachusetts General Hospital in 1818 and went on to form the first professional architectural office in the city.[37] Among the drawings for his unbuilt 1823 project for the Boston Athenaeum there is one which seems to be the earliest surviving local perspective by an architect other than Bulfinch (Cat. 10).[38] It harks back, through the latter's Hollis Street Church drawing, to Joshua Kirby.[39] Except for the addition of color washes, it shows nothing of the graphic strides made by Latrobe and his followers in the Quaker City.[40] The perspective from G.M. Dexter's office of his own house at Cottage Farm, to be dated as late as 1850 (Cat. 19), displays a more accomplished vocabulary of shades and shadows within the building itself and a faint hint of cloudy atmosphere, but no cast shadows, not even a horizon line, suggest the plane upon which it is to sit. The drawing differs from those by Bulfinch or Parris in that it is a two-point projection, but the presentation exhibits very little advance over Kirby's plates, some of which illustrate double vanishing points.

Not until 1856, apparently, do we find a local designer fully exploiting shades and shadows, landscape and staffage in a perspective. This is Joseph R. Richards's watercolor presentation of his project for remodeling Asher Benjamin's 1832 Joseph T. Buckingham house in Cambridge, a commission Richards won in competition with Elbridge Boyden and Phinehas Ball. Jack Quinan suggests that Buckingham picked his architect on the basis of his advanced graphics: "Where Boyden and Ball used flat washes and inked lines" on their elevation, Richards "depicts the house as a fully realized three-dimensional object in a lush landscaped setting."[41] Viewed in its historical context, this is a brilliant achievement, for it seems that otherwise it was not until after the Civil War that most local architects or their renderers caught up with the rest of the profession in graphic presentation.

Next to this conservative (not to say backward) string of graphics, the work of Hammatt Billings must appear an exception. Trained as an illustrator (with Abel Bowen, who published after-the-fact, wood-engraved views of Boston buildings[42]) as well an architect, he seems to have learned much from and carried into the 1830s and 1840s the methods of architectural presentation practiced locally in the 1820s by that "composer," A.J. Davis.[43] Billings, like Davis, recorded views of existing Boston landmarks for lithographers such as Pendleton & Co., who proliferated locally before the Civil War.[44] In addition, the sheet of drawings Billings seems to have executed in 1839 for an engraved publicity broadside of 1840 for Ammi Young's Boston Customs House (Cat. 11) shows that he was familiar with European neo-classical graphic styles as well. Both the exterior and interior views are in outline and unshaded, although ambience is indicated, and these are characteristics apparently otherwise unknown at this date in Boston but found in published graphics by Gilly, Weinbrenner, Schinkel, or Percier and Fontaine (or, in the figurative arts, Flaxman). As a jack-of-all-designs, and perhaps most importantly as a book illustrator (*Uncle Tom's Cabin*, 1852

and 1853), Billings, in any event, stands apart from his specialized professional colleagues in the architectural offices. He was more composer than builder (although he did both), who was at times called upon to provide exteriors for buildings planned by others, and, although his surviving graphics do not demonstrate the fact (Cat. 33a–c), he seems to have on occasion composed in perspective.[45]

Boston architectural graphics in general seem conservative through the first half of the nineteenth century. No rough perspective sketches (admittedly always the rarest of survivors from this era) such as we have from the hand of, say, Philadelphia's John Haviland, seem to exist. The inked orthographic presentation is the established fact of office practice, and only the frequent addition of even color washes distinguishes it from eighteenth-century work (Cat. 29). As we have noted, old-fashioned graphics presenting old-fashioned design ideas survive into the 1820s, as in the work of Solomon Willard (Cat. 9); in fact, this carries into mid-century (Cat. 28). Thereafter the use of perspective becomes routine.

Just as the study of eighteenth- and early nineteenth-century graphics adds to our understanding of changing style, so we learn much about the characteristics of picturesque eclecticism and Beaux-Arts classicism by considering the way post–Civil War architects shaped their works "on the boards." Orthographics survive as the prescribed method for classical composition and presentation, while perspective becomes common as the obvious mode for picturesque composition. In each case, however, a concern for the relationship between a building and its setting is eventually established as an integral part of the design process. The depiction of ambience in architectural presentation becomes common in the 1840s, after the perspective prescriptions of Alexander Jackson Davis published by Andrew Jackson Downing.[46] In Boston, in this collection, the first indication of place appears in a rendered elevation of 1843, bearing G.J.F. Bryant's name, for the Mt. Auburn Cemetery chapel in Cambridge (Cat. 24), but it was not until the picturesque era after the Civil War that rendered perspectives became a standard of office practice.

With the rise of competitive practice; the development of the architect as one who draws rather than builds and as one no longer rooted in the building trades; and the increasing availability of academic training, either here (at M.I.T. after 1868 [Cats. 55–56]) or abroad, attention to drawing as representative of the profession began to assume an importance it had not previously possessed. An article in the first volume of *The American Architect* (1876) suggests the altered training and position of the architect and consequent role of the architectural drawing since earlier in the century. It purposely omits discussion of "the necessary acquirements of the draughtsman in knowledge of work and of construction" in order to concentrate upon what "to expect of him when he undertakes to make a drawing for publication or exhibition."[47] "The good draughtsman must have the eye and feeling of an artist," the article goes on to say, and only extended training in drawing ornament and the figure will develop this.[48] Since "this ought to take a greater proportion of the learner's time than can be spared by the office student," it is obvious that the writer was recognizing the end of the system of apprenticeship in the trades or the drafting room and the beginning of academic and artistic training for the architect.

As this article also makes clear, this emphasis upon artistic drawing was encouraged by the development of the two arenas in which the architect could now routinely display his graphic skills: publications and exhibitions.[49] In 1876 Boston publisher James R. Osgood followed his short-lived *Architectural Sketch Book* (from 1873) with *The American Architect and Building News*, the country's first sustained professional periodical. Heliotypes after drawings of current designs appear in each issue (Cat. 40).[50] This outlet favored one medium over another, since the magazine in 1882 advised its contributors that a

drawing for reproduction "must be in line, on white paper, without tinting of any kind. . . . The best results are obtained by using black ink."[51] Such directions favored line over tone, pen and ink over watercolor, and reinforced the trend toward black-and-white line drawings which accompanied the evolution of the textured forms and surfaces of the Queen Anne, or shingle style (Cat. 46).[52]

The American Architect also reminded contributors that their audience was a professional one that could understand analytical diagrams, structural details, and other tectonic drawings, but perspectives nevertheless accounted for a large number of the illustrations it published in the last quarter of the nineteenth century. We must look hard to find scattered perspectives before the 1860s, and the ones we do find are more diagrammatic than artistic; they are difficult to avoid among the graphic remains of architects' offices after that date. This is true of both the design sketches, or "proofs," in which perspective is used to study an arrangement previously drawn orthographically (Cats. 37b–37c, 60), and the finished exhibition drawings (Cat. 63).

Drawings by architects had been part of the exhibitions of the Massachusetts Charitable Mechanic Association since the 1830s (*see* Cat. 11) and that practice continued through this era.[53] The new emphasis upon artistic presentation required a less trade-oriented venue, however, and this was provided by the Boston Art Club where in 1886, for example, two hundred and six drawings by English and American architects (the latter field apparently dominated by local designers) were hung for public display.[54] This exhibition appears to have contained nothing but presentation perspectives. The reviewer for *The American Architect* treated this as an art exhibition, although he did occasionally probe beyond line and color to criticize the designs of the buildings presented. Theodore Langerfeldt's perspective of an unidentified church (Cat. 39) may have been created for such an exhibition.

Increased opportunity for display provided by

both publication and exhibition generated more artistic renderings by the architectural profession of the post–Civil War years. Increased frequency of communication among architects and between architects and clients or prospective clients accounts for the development of an artistic facility with pen, pencil, or brush that went far beyond earlier achievement. Either the principal developed his own graphic skills or he hired draftsmen who specialized in "rendering" to produce eye-catching views of proposed buildings. Architects such as Robert Peabody (Cat. 67) or Bertram Goodhue (Cat. 75) were brilliant draftsmen in their own right; others hired professional presenters like Theodore Langerfeldt (Cat. 39), Samuel J. Brown (Cat. 49), or E. Eldon Deane.[55] Such hired hands became so much in demand that some of them, like Langerfeldt and Deane, abandoned the practice of architecture to become full-time artists, "perspectivists," or "renderers." It is only at this belated period that Boston draftsmen produced significant exemplars of Latrobe's legacy.

Artistic skills became so highly developed among local draftsmen of the last decades of the nineteenth century that Solomon Willard's characterization of the possibilities of misusing architectural representation became a reality. Already in 1825 he recognized that clever drawing could be used as a means of deceiving a client: "The purest design does not make the most catching picture," he wrote,[56] "and an artist who intends to succeed . . . should not draw what he thinks it proper to build, but what he thinks will please. The design should be light and fanciful and the drawing deceptive and highly colored." Following this line of reasoning, the Philadelphia architect Benjamin Linfoot in 1884 recommended "jaunty little perspective sketches" in pen and ink as a mode of architectural "picture-making" which "enables us to widen, lengthen, straighten and do what we will with almost any subject."[57] Abuse of the artist's skills in "correcting" the designer's mistakes by the early twentieth century led

some competition committees to limit the extent of such decorative overlay. The conditions written by Henry Holt for the Wellesley College dormitory competition of 1903 (Cat. 72) clearly recognized the problem. They stipulate the submission of, among other graphics, a bird's-eye perspective with "light indications of color and shadows, without accessories" (a rule that was later modified, it is true). The bird's-eye may have been chosen because it is an impossible view for a human and therefore a less seductive vision.

This restriction may also reflect the fact that draftsmen of this period who had been trained at the Ecole des Beaux-Arts had absorbed there not only a predisposition toward classical design, but also a prejudice against perspective projections, in favor of a return to orthographic purity (Cat. 71). The French, according to *The American Architect* of 1876, worked in "geometrical elevation rather than perspective; a treatment to which the style they work in is much better suited than the more irregular and picturesque manner of most English or American architects, which absolutely requires a perspective rendering."[58] H.H. Richardson's mistrust of drawings in general and his eschewing of perspective studies and presentations in favor of planimetric projections (Cats. 51–52) surely stem from his Ecole training.[59] It was, of course, Richardson's historical achievement to impose French discipline upon the Anglo-picturesque "excesses" of his era.

Picturesque, eclectic architecture required a fund of usable historical detail. Increasingly during the second half of the nineteenth century, architects trained themselves by studying the building of the past. They drew not only *for* buildings but also *from* buildings. Such after-the-fact graphics, when they are not commissioned for commercial reasons (as was the case earlier with Davis or Billings), are an essential part of the architect's educational process. Central to this category of architectural drawing is the travel sketch, a visual and manual coordinating of experience that, although it was more common before the advent of the portable roll film camera, is still practiced by inquisitive students. These graphics can tell the historian much about an architect's sources and preferences, or they can provide a key to the understanding of an entire period.

When, after the Civil War, American students began to journey to Paris for their education, the opportunity to experience at first hand the history of Western architecture frequently gave rise to numerous visual notes recording days spent on the road. The graphic remains of Robert Peabody (Cat. 64a–b), Clipston Sturgis (Cat. 68a–b), and Bertram Goodhue (Cat. 74) include impressive, on the spot perspective sketches of this sort. In the process of recreating in situ the architectural forms of the past, such student wayfarers amassed decorative vocabularies and stores of picturesque details which would later find echoes in the buildings they produced as mature, eclectic designers.

Local draftsmen also led the way in the study of the architectural history of their own country, a process that gave rise to the Colonial Revival in the 1870s.[60] The period began in 1863 with John Sturgis's measured drawings of the Hancock House on Beacon Hill[61] and continued in the work of a number of younger men, including Ogden Codman[62] and Herbert Browne. Profiles of the moldings Browne recorded in colonial and Federal houses along the North Shore (Cat. 61) no doubt found their way into fashionable middle-class homes of the greater Boston area in the years that followed.

Picturesque design is best studied in perspective sketches and best presented in rendered perspectives, but even where graphics remained flat on the sheet rather than illusionistically creating three dimensions, the post–Civil War draftsmen projected a more vibrant image than did their predecessors, through the manipulation of croquill pen or water-color brush. The contrast between Nathaniel Bradlee's ink drawing of a stick style house of the 1870s and William Preston's of a shingle house of the 1880s (Cats. 23, 46) is not merely one of stylistic progression. Trained in the apprenticeship system before 1850, Bradlee created a ruled ink elevation in a freehand perspective landscape that is brittle and dry compared with the work of Preston, who had at least a year's training at the Ecole des Beaux-Arts after 1860. Although also orthographic, the drawing of the Baldwin house is fluid rather than stiff, loose rather than tight, sinuous rather than angular, and fully evocative of the textural shingled forms that characterized the era to which it belongs.

The application of color to elevations shows the identical transformation. Sumner in 1819 used pale, even washes without shadows (Cat. 7); Isaiah Rogers in the 1840s cast shadows on evenly washed walls (Cat. 14); both were classicists. With the coming of the picturesque in architectural design, Impressionism in painting, and the quickened interest in watercolor as a medium evinced by the founding of the American Watercolor Society in New York in 1866–1867,[63] surface color begins to dance and sparkle across the Whatman paper. The draftsman in Luther Briggs's office who created the Thayer Public Library elevation used wash conservatively (Cat. 32), in keeping with its lingering classical details. Gridley Bryant's Agassiz Museum facade of around 1860 (Cat. 25), on the other hand, seems precocious in its use of mottled colors. Henry Hartwell and William Richardson's shingle style elevation (Cat. 57) or Arthur Rotch's study for the Wellesley College Art Museum (Cat. 59), both of the 1880s, are the norm. Even in details the change between the work of the first and the second half of the century is discernable: witness the contrast between the cool gray wash of the Bulfinchian capital of the 1820s (Cat. 3) and the soft pencil rendering of that for Preston's Society of Natural History Museum of the early 1860s (Cat. 42).

Architectural graphics are not, however, a matter of presentation alone. Once the design is established, the draftsman must, finally, create the instructions to get it built. As the decades passed, the architect found himself joining or hiring trained engineers or structural consultants and generating ever more multiple and detailed drawings due to a number of historical factors: He became increasingly removed from the building site; technology became sophisticated beyond eighteenth-century wooden spans and load-bearing masonry supports, with the introduction of structural masonry vaults in the neoclassical era and the gradual production of industrial materials such as terra cotta, plate glass, and rolled iron beams a few decades later (and, by the 1880s, steel beams); stylistic choice became enriched with the introduction of Gothic and other non–classical modes (including exotic, Near-Eastern forms) in the 1830s and 1840s; and types of buildings to be designed became more diverse in answer to the needs of an increasingly pluralistic society. The plan and upright of the era before 1820–1830 (Cat. 7) would no longer suffice. Latrobe's sophisticated graphics were necessary to explain complex vaulting and heating systems,[64] and by the end of his career even Bulfinch found it necessary to draw a vast number of sheets (one hundred survive) for the Maine State House (1829–32),[65] where only one had apparently sufficed for the earlier capitol of his native Commonwealth (Cat. 1). Increasingly, by the middle of the century and after, the drafting load upon the architect's office became heavier and heavier.

The graphic remains from the continuous offices of George Dexter and Nathaniel Bradlee (Cats. 17–23), like the drawings of other architectural firms, contain rich examples of detailed structural instructions made necessary by new building types (such as depots and roundhouses), the introduction of less familiar styles, and the new structural materials and techniques. The graphic clarity introduced by Latrobe is furthered in these models of communication through the use of conventional color coding of ma-

terials in ruled ink orthographics (Cat. 22) that are arranged into standard sequences beginning with plans, passing through elevations to framing diagrams, and ending with structural and other explanatory vignettes. Details and some framing diagrams were produced in the eighteenth and early nineteenth century (*see* Cat. 6), but now, from his distant drafting room, the architect felt compelled to indicate every floor joist and every chord of every roof truss in the most routine of commercial work (Cat. 17) as well as more monumental building (Cat. 37a), to detail graphically custom iron castings (Cat. 20); to dimension every stone and each pane of glass (Cat. 21); to visualize, in an apparently rare isometric projection, the joining of iron post with iron girder and beams in a commercial block (Cat. 22); and to draw constructional diagrams for pier footings (Cat. 50). What are left from the Dexter and Bradlee offices are bound gatherings, chronologically arranged by job, that form master sets from which copies could be traced for transportation to the building site. These seem to be the office records, the tidy chronicles of professional work executed over decades.

During mid-century, as the drawings from these mainstream professional offices attest, the standard of modern architectural working drawings was established. The graphic remains from a later practice, that of William G. Preston, affirm the continuity of graphic technique while they bear witness to ongoing changes (Cats. 42–47). Many of the drawings from this office are on translucent tracing paper rather than the heavy Whatman sheets that had been common since the previous century. The student witnesses the introduction of this now standard material in leafing through the remains of Bradlee's office, where increasingly from the late 1860s to early 1870s framing diagrams, at least, were executed on trace; a large portion of the drawings that remain from Preston's practice were also drawn on white translucent sheets. The reason for the switch is to be found, of course, in the introduction around 1870 of photocopying by means of blueprinting.[66] Where once copies could be generated only by the laborious hackwork of lowly tracers, a drawing could now be multiplied by using light. The process's limited ability to produce gradations of tone led to graphic simplification. The black ink drawing on translucent tracing paper or linen became the central architectural graphic form once sketching and presenting had achieved a design acceptable to the client. Here, Charles Parker's ink line drawings for the Congregational church in Chicopee of 1868 (Cat. 36a–d) represent early examples of the transformation (cf. George Clough's use of heavy paper for the drawings of his Methodist church in Malden, 1872 [Cat. 48a–c]), while the linen-based, orthographic working drawings of 1903 from the office of Cram, Goodhue and Ferguson for the Mather District School (Cat. 78a–c) represent the modern standard, largely unchanged until the recent introduction of computer-generated images. These diagrammatics, produced by an anonymous draftsman (or -men), reflect the corporate structure of the modern architectural office.

The foregoing notes are intended to place the following drawings within a historical context. That which finally emerges from this brisk general overview is the need for thorough scholarship in a number of areas within the subject of Boston, and, more generally, nineteenth-century American architectural drawings. To name just a few: the introduction and use of varieties of three-dimensional representation around 1800 (and their impact upon the characteristics of architectural style); the role of drawing in the process of architectural design; the introduction of new technology as witnessed in graphic remains; the drawing as index of developing professional and office procedure;[67] the identification and role of the renderer after the Civil War; the relationship between rendering and the history of painting and watercolor during the same period; the impact of

reproductive processes, from blueprinting to heliotype and beyond; and the changing role of the individual draftsman in the creation of corporate offices in the late nineteenth century. And, finally, more emphasis should be placed on the identification, collection, and preservation of these central documents of the history of American architecture. If this prolegomenon and catalogue suggest something of the richness and rewards that await the serious student of architectural drawings, and if ensuing research augments and emends any or all of the observations made here, they will have served their purpose.

NOTES

1. The relationship between drawings and ideals is the focus of James Pierce Smith, "Architectural Drawings and the Intention of the Architect," *Art Journal* 27, Fall 1967, 48–59; see also, James S. Ackerman, "Architectural Practice in the Italian Renaissance," *JSAH*, XIII, October 1954, 3–11, and Wolfgang Lotz, "The Rendering of the Interior in Architectural Drawings of the Renaissance," in his *Studies in Italian Renaissance Architecture*, Cambridge MA, 1977, 1–65.

2. For Rhode Island: William H. Jordy and Christopher P. Monkhouse, *Buildings on Paper: Rhode Island Architectural Drawings 1825–1945*, Providence, 1982; for Philadelphia: James F. O'Gorman et al., *Drawing Toward Building: Philadelphia Architectural Graphics, 1732–1986*, Philadelphia, 1986; for Worcester MA: Lisa Koenigsberg, *Renderings from Worcester's Past: Nineteenth-Century Architectural Drawings from the American Antiquarian Society*, Worcester, 1987.

3. For a guide to local surviving archival material, see Nancy Carlson Schrock, ed., *Architectural Records in Boston*, New York and London, 1983.

4. Among general histories of Boston architecture in the nineteenth century are: Walter H. Kilham, *Boston After Bulfinch*, Cambridge MA, 1946; Walter Muir Whitehill, *Boston: A Topographical History*, Cambridge MA, 2d ed., 1968; Douglass Shand Tucci, *Built in Boston: City and Suburb, 1800–1950*, Boston, 1978; Jane Holtz Kay, *Lost Boston*, Boston, 1980.

5. See David Gebhard and Deborah Nevins, *200 Years of American Architectural Drawings*, New York, 1977, and

Deborah Nevins and Robert A.M. Stern, *The Architect's Eye: American Architectural Drawings from 1799–1978*, New York, 1979.

6. For discussions of the variety of architectural graphics see my essay in O'Gorman *et al.*, *Drawing Toward Building*, 1 *et seq.*, and Pauline Saliga, "The Types and Styles of Architectural Drawings," in John Zukowsky *et al.*, *Chicago Architects Design*, Chicago, 1982, 20 *et seq.*

7. See Jack Quinan, "Some Aspects of the Development of the Architectural Profession in Boston between 1800 and 1830," *Old-Time New England*, LXVIII, July–December 1977, 32–37.

8. See William H. Pierson, Jr., *American Buildings and Their Architects. The Colonial and Neo-Classical Styles*, New York, 1976.

9. See Ernest Allen Connally, *Printed Books on Architecture 1485–1805*, Urbana IL, 1960, 21–24.

10. See Jeffrey A. Cohen's essay in O'Gorman *et al.*, *Drawing Toward Building*, 15–32.

11. Details occasionally occur, especially of stairs, whose complex geometry required plotting.

12. See *The Builder's Magazine: or, a Universal Dictionary for Architects*, London, 1788, *s.v.*, "Draught."

13. For a couple that do, see Anon., "John Singleton Copley's Houses on Beacon Hill, Boston," *Old-Time New England*, XXV, January 1935, 85–95, and Frederic C. Detweller, "Thomas Dawes's Church in Brattle Square," *Old-Time New England*, LXIX, Winter–Spring 1979, 1–17.

14. C.R. Lounsbury, "An Elegant and Commodious Building: William Buckland and the Design of the Prince William County Courthouse," *JSAH*, XXXXVI, September 1987, 228–240.

15. I have in mind specifically Jefferson's free-hand ink sketches housed in the Huntington Library in San Marino CA (*i.e.*, 9364 [1–4]); all are orthographic.

16. These include descriptive geometry, formulated by the French mathematician Gaspard Monge (1746–1818).

17. S.Y. Edgerton, *The Renaissance Rediscovery of Linear Perspective*, New York, 1975.

18. In particular, Brook Taylor, *Linear Perspective: or, a New Method of Representing Justly All Manner of Objects*, London, 1715; Joshua Kirby, *Dr. Brook Taylor's Method of Perspective Made Easy*, Ipswich, 1754; and Joshua Kirby, *The Perspective of Architecture*, London, 1761.

19. Harvard College acquired Kirby's edition of *Taylor's Method of Perspective* in 1765 (Harold Kirker, *The Architecture of Charles Bulfinch*, Cambridge MA, 1969, 4, n. 7). The Social Architectural Library of Boston about 1810 owned a number of the Taylor/Kirby publications, as did the Boston Athenaeum (see Quinan, "Development of the Architectural Profession"). The Athenaeum's 1810 catalogue also lists Thomas Malton's *Complete Treatise of Perspective*, 1779, and Edward Noble's *Elements of Perspective*, 1771 (I owe these bibliographical notes to Christopher Monkhouse). For the Athenaeum's edition of Kirby's *Perspective of Architecture*, see Cat. 10.

20. O'Gorman *et al.*, *Drawing Toward Building*, Catalogue 22. See note 14.

21. *The Builder's Magazine*, *s.v.*, "Design."

22. Kirker, *Bulfinch*, 287.

23. See James F. O'Gorman, *H.H. Richardson and His Office: Selected Drawings*, Cambridge MA, 1974, 18 *et seq.*

24. Fisk Kimball, *Thomas Jefferson, Architect*, Boston, 1916 (reprint, New York, 1968); Frederick Doveton Nichols, *Thomas Jefferson's Architectural Drawings*, Boston and Charlottesville, 1961.

25. Agnes A. Chichrist, "Notes for a Catalogue of the John McComb [Jr.] . . . Collection of Architectural Drawings in the New-York Historical Society," *JSAH*, XXVIII, October 1969, 201–210, and "John McComb, Sr. and Jr., in New York, 1784–1799," *JSAH*, XXXI, March 1972, 10–21.

26. Helen A. Cooper *et al.*, *John Trumbull. The Hand and Spirit of a Painter*, New Haven CT, 1982, 276–277 (notes by Egon Verheyen). See note 31.

27. Kirker, *Bulfinch*, 20.

28. One other early perspective should be noted, that awkward, amateurish production attributed to Benjamin Chew showing a preliminary design for Cliveden in Germantown, Philadelphia, 1763. See O'Gorman *et al.*, *Drawing Toward Building*, 2, 5. As misplaced early drawings come to light, the number of known perspectives from this era will certainly increase.

29. The "Principles" is a bound manuscript of 42 Whatman sheets roughly 15 × 9″ in the Library of Con-

gress. Ff. 1, 5, and 7 bear an 1813 watermark. It is identified as in the architect's hand by Ellen Susan Bulfinch, *The Life and Letters of Charles Bulfinch*, Boston, 1896, 84.

The date of this gathering is identical to what has been said to be the earliest American publication on perspective, Simeon De Witt's, *The Elements of Perspective*, Albany, 1813 (Charles B. Wood III, *American Architectural Books*, South Woodstock CT, 1984, #144). De Witt hopes to attract a readership broader than the profession, however: "The Author's principal aim . . . is, to have Perspective introduced among the studies of a liberal education. . . . He has taken some pains to make his subject an object of attention . . . [by] shewing the many respects in which it may have a wholesome influence on the morality and happiness, as well as on the usefulness of men as members of society" (from the preface). This was characteristic of the many books on the subject produced by Boston publishers during the century, such as the anonymous *Easy Lessons in Perspective* (Boston: Hilliard, Gray, Little and Wilkins, 1830) or Joseph Ropes's *Practical Perspective* (Portland and Boston, 1851), which were primarily textbooks for the young.

30. It should be noted that the series of mathematical theses directed by Professor Samuel Webber at Harvard College, spanning the years 1782 to 1839 (thus postdating Bulfinch's student days), contain many exercises in perspective construction, not a few of them based upon Bulfinch's works. Their production makes the scarcity of preserved perspectives from coeval architects's offices all the more curious. The theses are housed in Harvard Archives. See John P. Brown, "Notes on the Bulfinch Church at Lancaster, Mass.," *Old-Time New England*, XXVII, April 1937, 148–151.

31. Trumbull's 1777 drawing is a two-point perspective with shadows cast on the building but virtually no indication of the ground upon which it might sit. Two-point perspectives are also illustrated in Kirby.

32. Other than Bulfinch's, and one by Billings (Cat. 11), the only interior perspective in this collection is Thayer's presentation drawing for the Providence City Hall (Cat. 40). Some others were available for selection, but they were rare indeed. The exterior rendering is much more common.

33. O'Gorman *et al.*, *Drawing Toward Building*, 5.

34. See William H. Pierson, Jr., *American Buildings and Their Architects. Technology and the Picturesque, The Corporate and the Early Gothic Styles*, Garden City NY, 1978, 273–275.

35. Bulfinch, *Bulfinch*, 213 (7 January [1818]).

36. Richard B.K. McLanathan, "Bulfinch's Drawings for the Maine State House," *JSAH*, XIV, May 1955, 12–17.

37. Quinan, "Development of the Architectural Profession."

38. There is a set of seven drawings in the collection of Society for the Preservation of New England Antiquities pertaining to the so-called Elizur Wright house on Forest Street in Medford, Massachusetts (destroyed by 1929), which contains perspectives that might challenge this claim, but I think not. The collection remains a puzzler, but I add the following observations to the ongoing discussion.

There are two sheets that clearly stem from the early years of the nineteenth century. One, ruled ink and gray and green washes on heavy paper (watermark 1804), 19½ × 10¾″, shows the elevation and chamber and parlor floors of a four-square Federal house with cruciform central hall beneath cupola and four corner rooms. Inscription: "Drawn . . . by A. BENJAMIN." On the reverse (by a different or later hand?): "Benjamin and Randal [?] . . . Medford House." The second sheet, clearly later as it is closer to the house as built, ruled ink and watercolor washes on heavy paper, 10 × 15¾″, shows a slightly varied elevation of the same house with a shed added to the right. Inscription: "Drawn by Thomas Rundle Boston." There is no watermark and no other indication of date (*contra* Richard Radis, "Thomas Rundle, Housewright," *Old-Time New England*, LXII, October–December 1971, 53–56). Given the relative reputations of the two men associated with the project, we might conclude that Benjamin established the design (in fact a generic domestic format of the period) and Rundle fiddled with it.

The remaining sheets in the collection are our chief interest in this context. They contain an astonishing series of perspective views of the house and shed and its extensive garden (see *Antiques*, March 1986, 606, pl. 1). They may be divided into two groups on the basis of sheet size, style, and variations in the details of the house. The first, two sheets containing pencil and watercolor drawings on heavy paper roughly 8 × 12″, shows a building significantly different in details from the Benjamin-Rundle design. The second, three sheets containing watercolor drawings on heavy paper, roughly 10 × 17″, that were clearly executed by another hand, shows alterations in the garden and details slightly varied from the second group (in fact, closer to the original design).

Everything we know about architectural drawing in Federal Boston argues against a very early date for these perspectives. They were perhaps executed as early as the 1820s by a visiting "composer" such as A.J. Davis, but firm documentation must be present if they are to be attributed to a local architect working in the first or second decades of the century.

That other perspectives were drawn in the early nineteenth century we know from literary rather than graphic sources. See Solomon Willard.

39. Parris could have used the copy of Kirby's *Perspective* in the Athenaeum, which inscriptions indicate comes from the library of Ithiel Town and was presented by Asher Benjamin in March 1810 (Cat. 10).

40. How long this presentation of buildings isolated on the sheet persists locally may be gauged from the ruled ink perspective of Luther Briggs and Company's unbuilt 1871 project for the Thayer Public Library in Braintree, Massachusetts (Cat. 32), in the collection at the Society for the Preservation of New England Antiquities.

41. Jack Quinan, "The Transformation of an Asher Benjamin House," *Antiques*, CXXII, August 1982, pl. III and p. 291.

42. *Bowen's Picture of Boston*, 1829 (2d ed., 1833).

43. Pierson, *Corporate and Early Gothic Styles*, 275–277. See note 46.

44. See also note 46. Billings's work as a "vedutist" remains uncatalogued, but see James F. O'Gorman, "H. and J.E. Billings of Boston," *JSAH*, XLII, March 1983, 56, n. 7.

45. O'Gorman, "Billings of Boston," 65: "When he was asked to draw a design for the exterior of . . . [the Tremont Street M.E. Church, Boston, 1860–1862, by Woodcock and Meacham], he walked to the . . . lot. Standing on the corner, he drew upon a piece of paper, resting upon his hat, the outline of the structure." This seems to be a prototype of that "pictorial vision" Vincent Scully remarked as a characteristic of later, shingle-style composition. He quotes the architect Ferdinand Von Beren of New Haven on perspective composition: "I'd get the picture and then work on the plan" (*The Shingle Style*, New Haven CT, 1955, 86).

46. A.J. Downing, *A Treatise on the Theory and Practice of Landscape Gardening, Adapted to North America*, New York and London, 1841, followed by *Cottage Residences*, 1842, and *The Architecture of Country Houses*, 1850.

Locally, the Downing-Davis visualizations first influenced a publication of 1845: *Views, with Ground Plans, of the Highland Cottages at Roxbury, (Near Boston,) Designed and Erected by Wm. Bailey Lang, Boston*. This contains "Scenic Views" of the houses lithographed by J.H. Bufford after drawings by Hammatt Billings. They reappear in Mrs. L.C. Tuthill's *History of Architecture*, Philadelphia, 1848.

47. "Architectural Drawing," *AABN*, I, 19 February 1876, 58–59.

48. Cf. the unsigned article entitled "The Value of Drawing from Life to the Architect," *Technology Architectural Review*, II, 12 October 1889, 34. The *Review* was a publication of the Massachusetts Institute of Technology.

49. See George E. Thomas's essay in O'Gorman, *et al.*, *Drawing Toward Building*, 117–125.

50. For a study of these illustrations see Eileen Michels, "Late Nineteenth-Century Published American Perspective Drawing," *JSAH*, XXXI, December 1972, 291–308.

51. *AABN*, XI, 25 February 1882, 95. Although Osgood's heliotype press could reproduce watercolor or wash drawings (and did, see, for example, the Eidlitz-Olmsted-Richardson project for the Albany State House, *AABN*, I, 11 March 1876, 85, and illustrations), the overwhelming majority of plates in the early years of the *AABN* were after line drawings.

52. Michels, "Published American Perspective Drawing," 291–308; William Hubbard, *Complicity and Convention*, Cambridge MA, 1980, 15–49.

53. *AABN*, IV, 2 November 1878, 149.

54. "The Boston Exhibition of Architectural Drawings,"

AABN, XIX, 13 and 27 March 1886, 124–125, 151–152. See also *AABN*, V, 17 May 1879, 159, and Michels, "Published American Perspective Drawing," 294, 296–297.

55. See Michels, "Published American Perspective Drawing," for Brown, Deane, and other hired pencils. Deane figures prominently in the pages of *AABN*, but no original work by him came to light during the preparation of this exhibition. For examples of his skill see Scully, *Shingle Style*, figs. 75–76, 81, etc.

56. William W. Wheildon, *Memoir of Solomon Willard, Architect*, Boston, 1865, 72–73 (11 April 1825, in a letter to the Bunker Hill Monument Association).

57. Benjamin Linfoot, *Architectural Picture Making with Pen and Ink*, Philadelphia, 1884, 5–13; Michels, "Published American Perspective Drawing," 300–301; O'Gorman *et al.*, *Drawing Toward Building*, 8.

58. *AABN*, I, 19 February 1876, 59.

59. Mariana Griswold Van Rensselaer, *Henry Hobson Richardson and his Works*, Boston, 1888, 119, 141; O'Gorman, *Selected Drawings*, 26.

60. William B. Rhoads, *The Colonial Revival*, New York, 1977.

61. Margaret Henderson Floyd, "Measured Drawings of the Hancock House by John Hubbard Sturgis," in A.L. Cummings, ed., *Architecture in Colonial Massachusetts*, Boston, 1979, 87–111.

62. See National Academy of Design, *Ogden Codman and the Decoration of Houses*, New York, 1988.

63. Kathleen A. Foster, *Makers of the American Watercolor Movement: 1860–1890*, Ann Arbor MI, 1982, 25–40. The Society's exhibitions flourished in the 1870s, when even architects participated in them.

64. O'Gorman *et al.*, *Drawing Toward Building*, 6.

65. McLanathan, "Maine State House," 12–17; Kirker, *Bulfinch*, 355.

66. A.O. Halse, "A History of the Developments in Architectural Drafting Techniques," D.Ed. diss., New York University, 1952, 402 *et seq*. Although the principle of blueprinting was discovered in the 1840s, as late as 1878 the *AABN* (IV, 3 August, 44) was describing it as if it were something new in office practice. See Nathaniel J. Bradlee.

67. One local model exists in this area: Jean A. Follett-Thompson, "The Business of Architecture: Williams Gibbons Preston and Architectural Professionalism in Boston during the Second Half of the Nineteenth Century," Ph.D. diss., Boston University, 1986.

Catalogue

Charles Bulfinch
(1763–1844)

Bulfinch's biography exemplifies the transition from eighteenth-century dilettante to nineteenth-century professional architect. He was born in Boston to a family of substance, educated at Harvard (Class of 1781), and "cultivate[d] a taste for Architecture" during idle moments in the employ of the merchant Joseph Barrell. He spent the years 1785–1787 traveling in England, France, and Italy, particularly "observing the wonders of Architecture." Returning to a town of some 15,000 population, he "passed a season of leisure, pursuing no business but giving gratuitous advice in architecture." A trip to New York and Philadelphia in 1788 informed him of the latest developments in those cultural centers.

His career as designer began in the middle 1780s with his project for the Massachusetts State House and his design for the Hollis Street Church (Fig. 2). The next decade brought both success and failure, in that he was elected to the Boston Board of Selectmen (1791), served as its Chairman from 1799 to 1817, and gave increasingly more advice in matters architectural, as for the Connecticut State House, Hartford, 1792. His project for a unified row of domestic buildings on Franklin Place, from 1793, brought London sophistication to Boston but eventually ruined him financially. From its failure Bulfinch was forced to charge for his services; as his wife wrote, "Architecture [became] his business, as it had been his pleasure."

Bulfinch transformed his native town through civic, domestic, ecclesiastical, and public projects; he found Boston largely a town of brick and left it a place of granite, ready to assume the stature of a city. He moved to Washington, D.C., late in 1817 to take on the duties of the architect of the federal Capitol, leaving Alexander Parris (*see*) to supervise his design for the Massachusetts General Hospital. Returning to Boston in 1830, he lived out his last years in retirement.

Bulfinch's graphic remains are numerous, although not as richly preserved as those of his older contemporary, Thomas Jefferson. They are scattered among a number of collections, including those of Harvard University, the New York Public Library, the Boston Athenaeum, the Massachusetts Historical Society, and elsewhere. For the Maine State House there is preserved an extraordinary set of one hundred sheets.

REFERENCES: Ellen S. Bulfinch, *The Life and Letters of Charles Bulfinch*, Boston, 1896; Charles A. Place, *Charles Bulfinch, Architect and Citizen*, Boston and New York, 1925; Richard B.K. McLanathan, "Bulfinch's Drawings for the Maine State House," *JSAH*, XIV, May 1955, 12–17; Harold Kirker, *The Architecture of Charles Bulfinch*, Cambridge MA, 1969.

1. MASSACHUSETTS STATE HOUSE, BOSTON, 1787, 1795–1798 (with later additions and restorations).

"Elevation and plan of the principal Story of the New State House in Boston," undated. Signed: "Chs Bulfinch." Sepia ink and gray wash on heavy (Whatman) paper; 11¹⁵/₁₆ × 9³/₁₆″. I.N. Phelps Stokes Collection, Miriam & Ira D. Wallach Division of Art, Prints, and Photographs; The New York Public Library; Astor, Lenox, and Tilden Foundations.

Bulfinch responded to calls for a place of assemblage for the Massachusetts General Court on 5 November 1787 with "a plan for a new State-house," but his project was not adopted until 16 February 1795 when he, Thomas Dawes of the Senate (a bricklayer-builder by trade), and Edward Robbins of the House were appointed agents to execute his design. The building was occupied early in 1798.

Kirker has written that "the plan accepted in 1795 was either the same or substantially the same as that submitted in 1787." Whether this drawing stems from the earlier or the later year (both dates have been mentioned in the literature; the latter is accepted by Kirker and Pickens), it assumes a key position not only as one of the earliest preserved documents in the history of Boston architectural graphics but also as a transitional work.

The drawing is recognized as a product of the architect's early career by the tentative quality of some of the draftsmanship, such as single lines representing interior partitions and the asymmetrical position of the central doorway of the third level in relation to the bay in which it is placed. The drawing is at first glance a characteristic eighteenth-century graphic combining "ichnography," or plan, with "orthography," or elevation, with no indication of the environment for which it was designed. Lines ruled with a drafting pen create geometrical diagrams of a kind that can be traced back in the few surviving eighteenth-century American drawings to the parchment representation of the Pennsylvania State House, Philadelphia ("Independence Hall"), of 1732, the oldest datable graphic from the era. But closer inspection reveals that this was probably not intended to be a directive for workmen at the site. This is more "presentation" than "work-

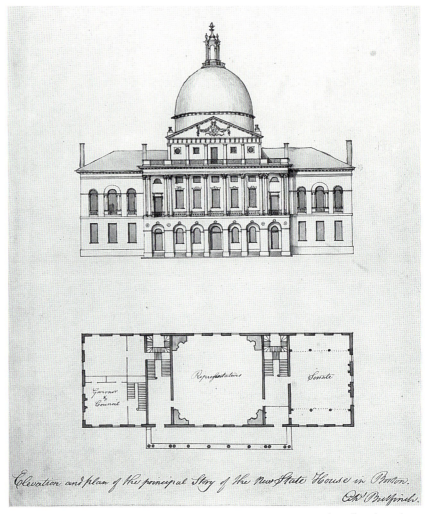

Elevation and plan of the principal Story of the New State House in Boston.
Chs Bulfinch.

1 (see also plate 1)

ing" drawing. There are no dimensions, the three windows shown in the front wall of the plan of the House do not correspond to the five shown in elevation, and, despite the lack of any indication of place, Bulfinch tried to capture something of the look of the finished product. He endeavored to achieve some sense of plasticity by

overlaying his orthography with shadows cast from a light source to the left and by washes manipulated to suggest the roundness of his dome, the projection of the central salient, and the free-standing position of the row of columns of the portico of the principal (second) floor. The visual quality of the sheet is further enhanced by the

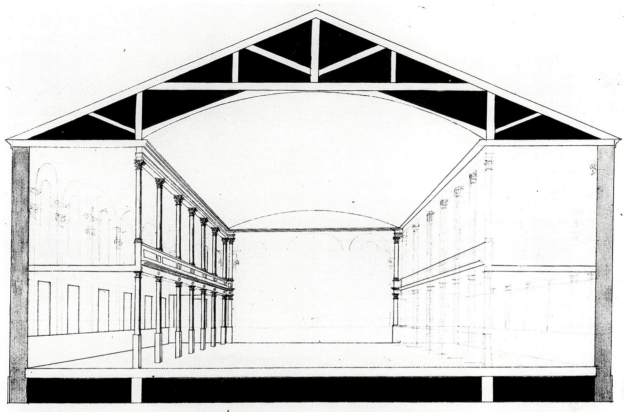

Interior of New North Church, Boston

2

use of sepia for lines and shadows and gray wash for windows, roof, and dome: a subtle shift in tone that gives life to the graphic (and is killed in black-and-white reproduction). The drawings for the Maine State House, 1829, are mature descendants of this sheet in number, design, and graphic style.

Clearly Bulfinch is striving here to transform the plan-and-upright, geometric diagram into a thing of visual appeal, just as he seems here to strive hesitantly toward a more plastic con-

ception of building form that he would eventually achieve in his last Boston works.

REFERENCES: I.N. Phelps Stokes and Daniel C. Haskell, *American Historical Prints . . . From the Phelps Stokes and Other Collections*, New York, 1933, 35; Harold Kirker, "Bulfinch's Design for the Massachusetts State House," *Old-Time New England*, LV, Fall 1964, 43–45; Kirker, *Bulfinch*, 101–113; Buford Pickens, "Wyatt's Pantheon, the State House in Boston and a New

View of Bulfinch," *JSAH*, XXIX, May 1970, 124–131.

2. NEW NORTH CHURCH (NOW ST. STEPHEN'S), HANOVER STREET, BOSTON, 1802–1804.

"Interior of New North Church, Boston" (transverse section with interior in perspective), undated. Unsigned. Graphite, black ink, and gray and terra-cotta washes on heavy paper, 9 1/16 × 15 1/16". Prints and Photographs Division, Library of Congress.

The cornerstone of this North End structure was laid in September 1802, and the *Columbian Centinel* of 5 May 1804, in an article noticing its dedication three days earlier, says that it "reflects honor upon the professional talents of the architect, *Charles Bulfinch.*" It goes on to describe a two-storied interior with Doric columns at the first level ("solid base") and Corinthian above ("highest place").

This unfinished drawing is a combination structural section and interior perspective. The overhead wood truss rests upon the interior rows of superimposed columns, while the sloping roof extends to the brick side walls. Bulfinch has used his gray wash to indicate areas beyond the vision of a visitor within the building (although not with complete consistency: the thickness of the shallow central vault reads as continuous with the interior). Yet there is little attempt to characterize accurately the ambience within: the viewpoint is an impossible one outside the space, and color is used diagrammatically rather than optically.

This one-point construction is akin to examples of perspective method contained in Bulfinch's manuscript "Principles of Perspective," now in the Library of Congress, undated but containing at least three sheets of Whatman paper watermarked 1813. Ff. 28–29 demonstrate the different results of drawing a one-point perspective of the interior of a church when the vanishing point is on or off center (Fig. 3). The interior perspective remains an infrequent graphic in nineteenth-century Boston (*see* Cats. 11 and 40).

REFERENCE: Kirker, *Bulfinch,* 168–172.

3

3. UNITED STATES CAPITOL, WASHINGTON, D.C., 1792 *et seq.* (Bulfinch in charge, 1817–1829).

Diagrammatic plan and rendered elevation of a Composite capital, undated. Unsigned. Ink and wash on heavy paper, 15 × 13¼" (irregular).

Prints and Photographs Division, Library of Congress.

This drawing is preserved among the Bulfinch material relating to the federal Capitol at the Library of Congress. Its date and intended location are open to speculation. Its quality as

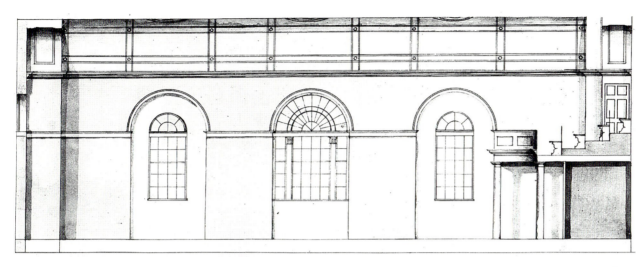

4

a drawing is not, and seems beyond the capacity of Bulfinch himself. We know he was assisted by draftsmen in the Capitol architect's office, including Solomon Willard (*see*); this drawing probably stems from one of the team.

4. UNITARIAN CHURCH, WASHINGTON, D.C., 1821–1822 (demolished 1900).

Lateral interior elevation, undated. Unsigned. Ink and colored washes, 10½ × 14½″. Prints and Photographs Division, Library of Congress.

Bulfinch designed his last ecclesiastical commission in 1821, and the structure was dedicated in June of the next year. The Library of Congress has a set of drawings for this building, originally bound in a folio entitled "Plans &c for the Unitarian Church at Washington. 1821–1822," which includes site and floor plans, variant interior and exterior elevations, and details.

This is a shaded orthographic drawing of the side wall of the barrel-vaulted sanctuary, from gallery over the entrance to pulpit niche, which, like other drawings in the set, carries on the eighteenth-century orthographic mode.

REFERENCES: Kirker, *Bulfinch*, 341–346; Deborah Nevins and Robert A.M. Stern, *The Architect's Eye: American Architectural Drawings from 1799–1978*, New York, 1979, 52–53.

Asher Benjamin (1772/1773–1845)

Benjamin's career spanned the Federal and Greek Revival eras. Through his numerous publications he spread the innovations of Bulfinchian design to the farther reaches of New England and the near west and south. We know he was born in Hartland, Connecticut, but his early life and training are a mystery. By his mid-twenties Benjamin was working as a housewright on buildings in various locations in the Connecticut River valley. By 1795 his skills had reached a level at which he "made the drawings and superintended the erection of a circular staircase in the State House at Hartford" (a design by Bulfinch). His *Country Builder's Assistant*, which appeared at Greenfield, Massachusetts, in 1797, was the first architectural publication by an American (earlier books had been editions of English works). This contained the Bulfinch-derived plate 33, plan, elevations, section, and detail of the pulpit of the generic, New England Federal meeting house. It inspired the designers of religious structures from Maine to Ohio and beyond.

Benjamin appears in Boston directories as a housewright by 1802. Bulfinch continued to influence his work in buildings and in books, as witnessed by his West Church, Cambridge Street, Boston, and his *American Builder's Companion*, both of 1806. Benjamin produced five more books, the last appearing in 1843, in all publishing seven titles in 47 revised editions to 1856. In these the more robust Greek Revival gradually replaced the lighter, Roman-based Federal details of his early career. He continued to design buildings and monuments in and out of Boston (some 50 structures have been catalogued), although from 1810 to 1828 he also worked as a merchant and a real estate and manufacturing agent in both Boston and Nashua, New Hampshire.

In 1802 Benjamin advertised an architectural school at Windsor, Vermont. This may never have operated, but he apparently did take apprentices, such as Hammatt Billings (*see*), at least in the 1820s and 1830s. These educational activities plus his numerous publications rank Benjamin as a prime force in the development of early nineteenth-century architecture in New England and beyond.

Benjamin's few surviving drawings are scattered through public and private collections in New England and elsewhere.

REFERENCES: Jack Quinan, "The Architectural Style of Asher Benjamin," Ph.D. diss., Brown University, 1973; Jack Quinan, ed., "Asher Benjamin and American Architecture," *JSAH*, XXXVIII, October 1979, 244–270; Jack Quinan, "The Transformation of an Asher Benjamin House," *Antiques*, CXXII, August 1982, 288–292; Abbott Lowell Cummings, "Benjamin, Asher," *MEA*, I, 176–179.

5. FRONTISPIECE FOR AN UNIDENTIFIED BUILDING, 1797.

Elevation of an "Ionick Front," "Greenfield 4th of March 1797."

6

Signed: "A Benjamin." Black ink and gray wash on heavy paper, 9¼ × 6″. Society for the Preservation of New England Antiquities.

A six-panel door surmounted by a fan light and flanked by engaged half-columns supporting a triangular pediment, this is a characteristic Federal frontispiece. The fact that the shadows are cast by a sun placed upper right rather than the more conventional left may suggest the work of a neophyte draftsman. Except for those shadows (and the Ionic rather than Doric order) this might be a drawing for one of the doorways in plate 12 of Benjamin's *Country Builder's Assistant*, published the year he dated this sheet. The shadows add body to the usually flat orthography.

6. UNIDENTIFIED MEETING HOUSE, 1810.

Front elevation of a meeting house, "Drawn . . . by Asher Benjamin 1810." Black ink and gray and green washes on heavy paper (watermark 1808), 16¾ × 11″. (Flap attached to verso with brief description: "[Meeting] House 17 by 80 feet with a porch in front projecting 18 ft from house & 38 feet front. 4 courses of hammered Stone one foot each. Brick wall 31 feet high & 20 inches thick. 18 windows 16 lights of glass each of 18 by 11 Inches. 21 [windows] 24 lights each of glass 11 by 15 inches." On verso of flap: "Mr Lincoln.") Society for the Preservation of New England Antiquities.

This is one of a set of drawings preserved for this generic meeting house; there are also plans and framing diagrams. This orthographic projection composed of thin, ruled ink lines without indication of ambience, despite the presence of tentative wash shadows, is akin to the wood-engraved illustrations in Benjamin's contemporary books. These graphics, which contain major dimensions plus brief specifications, were all that was needed to erect a building in an era of traditional technology. Compare this with Sumner's drawing for the spire of the church at Peterborough, New Hampshire (Cat. 8).

REFERENCE: Deborah Nevins and Robert A.M. Stern, *The Architect's Eye: American Architectural Drawings from 1799–1978*, New York, 1979, 40–41.

Thomas W. Sumner (1768–1849)

Thomas Waldron Sumner, the son of a housewright, was born in Boston. First notice of his following in his father's footsteps comes from 1793. By 1800 he was a member of the Massachusetts Charitable Mechanic Association, for whom he designed an unbuilt meeting hall in 1802, and in 1804 he was a founding member of the Society of Associated Housewrights, where he served as president from 1808 to 1817 and from 1822 to 1823. Among other members was Asher Benjamin (*see*). From 1805 to 1811, and again in 1816 and 1817, he served as representative to the Massachusetts General Court, thus following Thomas Dawes and Charles Bulfinch (*see*) in combining building practice with political activity.

Except for several documented contacts with the younger Alexander Parris (*see*), we know little about Sumner's architectural activities other

than what we learn from drawings and projects such as those discussed below. In 1817 he drafted a set of plans of Asher Benjamin's Exchange Coffee House, Boston, 1806, and in 1824 he designed the East India Marine Hall (now part of the Peabody Museum) as well as the Independent Congregational Church (demolished), both in Salem. His last known work was the South Congregational Church at Washington and Castle streets, Boston, of 1827 (demolished). Thereafter he may have shifted his interests to business.

The few identified drawings by Sumner are held by the Essex Institute and the Peabody Museum, Salem, the Boston Athenaeum, the Bostonian Society, Harvard University Archives, and the Society for the Preservation of New England Antiquities.

REFERENCES: A biographical sketch of Sumner by Christopher P. Monkhouse is in Philip Chadwick Foster Smith, *East India Marine Hall: 1824–1974*, Salem, 1974, n.p.; Jack Quinan, "The Boston Exchange Coffee House," *JSAH*, XXXVIII, October 1979, 256–262.

7. SUFFOLK COUNTY BUILD-INGS, LEVERETT STREET, BOS-TON, 1819 (unbuilt competition entry).

"Elevation of the County Buildings on Leverett Street," "December 1819." "Drawn . . . by ⅄." Ink and watercolor on heavy paper, 19¼ × 27½". Society for the Preservation of New England Antiquities.

The history of the Leverett Street buildings, which included county court room and offices, keeper's house, and criminals' and debtors'

prisons, begins with a competition in 1819 which was won by Alexander Parris (*see*). Among the other competitors was, according to Zimmer, Charles Bulfinch, then resident in Washington. Parris's drawings for the keeper's house, seven sheets bound in marbleized covers, are at the Bostonian Society. Construction began in 1821, and Parris's buildings were occupied in 1822 and demolished in 1851.

This is one of the set of preserved drawings comprising Sumner's competition entry. Although they are signed only with an otherwise unknown device, it is possible to assign them to Sumner on the basis of his signature appearing on the paper which once bound them. An orthographic projection of ruled ink lines, only the even color wash distinguishes this from the drawings of Bulfinch or Benjamin. With court and keeper's house in the central block crowned by an axial cupola, and prisons in symmetrically placed outbuildings at right angles to the main structure, Sumner's project is stylistically as conservative as his graphics. It continues the Palladian schema of American public buildings reaching back to Philadelphia's Independence Hall group and beyond. Even Parris's winning design—judging by the drawings at the Bostonian Society, which combine granite forms with a Federal doorway—seems to have been stylistically conservative, that is, halfway between his Portland roots and his current Boston work.

REFERENCES: Monkhouse in Smith, *East India*, n.p.; Edward F. Zimmer, *The Architectural Career of Alexander Parris*, Ann Arbor, 1985, 422–433.

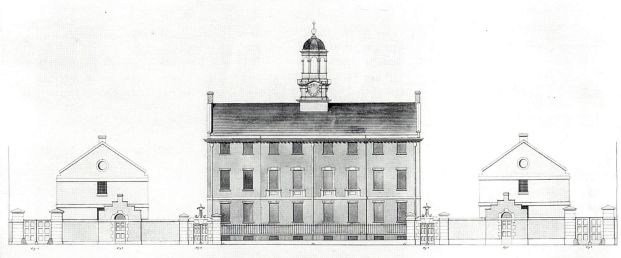

Fig 1. is the Gate which leads to the Criminals Yard.
Fig 2. Watch house or Constables Office.
Fig 3. is the Gate to enter the Court House.
Fig 4. is the Gate by which the Keeper enters his premises
Fig 5. is the Keepers Office
Fig 6. is the Gate which leads to the Debtors Yard.

Elevation of the County Buildings in Leverett Street

The Basement Story 10 feet
The Principal ...... 18 feet   } in the Clear
The first Chamber - 11 feet
The Upper ...... 9 feet

Plans ½ by ¼ Dimensions to a Scale of 9 feet to an inch by T.D.
December 1827

7 (see also plate 2)

8. UNITARIAN CHURCH, PETERBOROUGH, NEW HAMPSHIRE, 1825.

Elevation of a steeple, "Feb 8, 1825." "Drawn . . . / By Thoms W Sumner / Boston—No 3 Merchants Row." Ruled ink and gray, pale yellow, and light green washes on heavy paper, 12¾ × 7". Society for the Preservation of New England Antiquities; gift of Earle G. Shettleworth, Jr., 1987.

This recently discovered drawing was identified by Stephen Jerome as representing, line for line, the spire of the Peterborough church, a building Tolles dates between 1819 and 1825. As Tolles notes, the design has been attributed to Bulfinch, although he would assign it to an unknown architect, and it stems from the 1820 edition of Benjamin's *American Builder's Companion*. The tower seems to have been adapted from that shown in plate A of that guide, and this drawing would seem to fix firmly the date and the name of the draftsman of that crowning feature of the building at least.

Although drawn from the latest source—Bulfinch's style as promulgated by Benjamin—Sumner's design, like his drafting, follows eighteenth-century tradition (*see* Cat. 6). The Wren–Gibbs ecclesiastical formula is presented in a shaded orthography thoroughly characteristic of Sumner's other graphic work. The tower is lightly tinted in pale (faded?) yellow, the louvered openings are green, and the gray wash on the spire emphasizes the forward plane, creating a slight illusion of plasticity. Shading distinguished this from Benjamin's meeting house elevation of fifteen years earlier (Cat. 6).

8

REFERENCES: Bryant F. Tolles, Jr., *New Hampshire Architecture. An Illustrated Guide*, Hanover, 1979, 110–111; Earle G. Shettleworth, Jr., to author, 29 February 1988.

Solomon Willard (1783–1862)

Willard was born in Petersham, Massachusetts, and received early training in carpentry and cabinetmaking from his father. He moved to Boston in 1804, and in the following years he was associated as carpenter and carver with Peter Banner (Park Street Church), Asher Benjamin (*see*), Bulfinch (*see*), Parris (*see*), and Isaiah Rogers (*see*). He also traveled to and worked in Providence, New York, Philadelphia, Baltimore, and Washington, D.C.

Willard's aspirations apparently went far beyond the mechanical trades. According to his nineteenth-century biographer, "He early provided himself with the most approved works on architecture and perspective drawing; purchased an Encyclopaedia . . . and paid for his tuition at a drafting academy for at least two terms," and, before the end of the 1810s, "architectural drawing, carving in wood, various studies in chemistry and geology, teaching in drawing and perspective" occupied his time. In the 1820s, according to the same source, he "received pupils at his studio near St. Paul's Church, and gave lessons in architecture and drawing." (These are tantalizing glimpses of graphic instruction in early nineteenth-century Boston, a subject about which we know too little.) Despite such a busy schedule of work, study, and teach-

ing, he found time to visit the sculptor William Rush in Philadelphia and to assist Bulfinch with the presentation of his designs for the federal Capitol in 1818.

The design and superintendence of the Bunker Hill Monument in Charlestown, 1825–1842, remained his most important achievement. In that endeavor he opened the granite quarries at Quincy and developed processes of excavating, handling, and transporting the stone.

Few Willard drawings survive; they are distributed over a number of repositories. The drawings for the Bunker Hill Monument are at the American Antiquarian Society, Worcester, Massachusetts.

REFERENCES: William Wilder Wheilden, *Memoir of Solomon Willard, Architect and Superintendent of the Bunker Hill Monument*, [Boston], 1865; Jack Quinan, "Some Aspects of the Development of the Architectural Profession in Boston Between 1800 and 1830," *Old-Time New England*, LXVIII, July–December 1977, 32–37.

9. DIVINITY HALL, HARVARD COLLEGE, CAMBRIDGE, MASSACHUSETTS, 1825 (unbuilt project).

"Plan," "2d Floor" plan, and elevation, "Boston Sept 2nd 18[25?]." Signed: "S. Willard Delineator." (On verso: "Willards plan of Divinity College with wings & piazzas.") Ink and washes with graphite notes and emendations on heavy paper (later note: "Water Mark, 1819"), 19 × 25⅝″. Harvard University Archives.

Divinity Hall, erected in 1825, was the first Harvard building to stand

outside of the Yard. The commission was given to Willard about the time he was retiring from active architectural practice (to supply stone for the Bunker Hill Monument). Bunting and Floyd suggest that this drawing may be the work of Isaiah Rogers (*see*), who was then in his office. For the same reason, perhaps, Thomas Sumner (*see*) was given charge of the work and apparently modified the design. His drawing for the hall, also in Harvard Archives, shows a different scheme for the same project (it is on a sheet of Whatman paper of identical size as Willard's) but does not represent the finished building. That appears in a third drawing, dated 1834 and signed by William Sparrell, also in Harvard Archives. The purpose of the latter drawing remains unexplained.

Although they reflect similar concepts, Sumner's project is a planar pedimented pavilion with roots in the eighteenth century, while Willard's design is a stylistic hybrid. His building stretches 350 feet from end to end. The elevation shows a two-story arcuated central block 80 feet wide that reflects the heavier classicism of Bulfinch's late local works. It contains a chapel and commons at the second level. This is flanked by four-story residential wings that are decidedly eighteenth-century in scale, fronted by a one-story, colonnaded "Piazza." As built, smaller than either Willard's or Sumner's design, with the piazzas giving way to Greek Doric porticoes in front of the flanking entrances, the building reflected a further stylistic advance. This cannot be easily attributed to Sumner; the complete explication of this building's history remains to be unfolded.

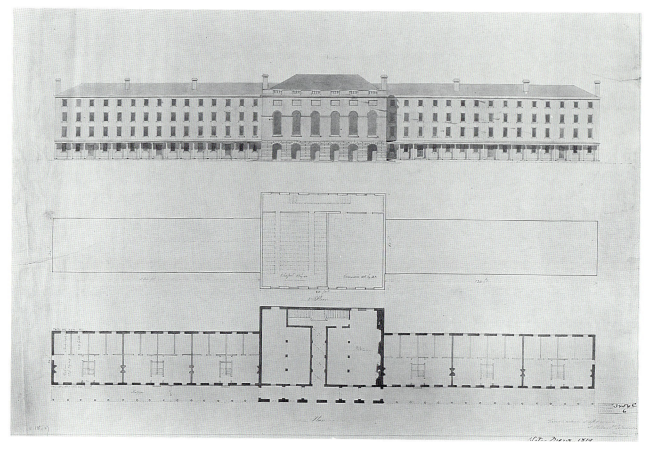

9

Neither Sumner's nor Willard's (nor, for that matter, Sparrell's) drawing shows a significant advance over eighteenth-century orthographics.

REFERENCE: Bainbridge Bunting (completed and edited by Margaret Henderson Floyd), *Harvard. An Architectural History*, Cambridge MA and London, 1985, 52–54, 293 note 41.

Alexander Parris (1780–1852)

Born in Halifax, Massachusetts, Parris was apprenticed to a housewright in Pembroke in his teens. He moved to Portland, Maine, in 1801, then to Richmond, Virginia, where between 1810 and 1812 he saw the works of Jefferson, Latrobe, and Mills. After service as captain of artificers during the War of 1812, he settled in Boston in 1815, and in 1818, established the

town's first professional architectural office. Among his early local works were the supervision of Bulfinch's design for the Massachusetts General Hospital, 1818–1823, and his own design for St. Paul's Tremont Street, 1819–1820.

Parris began his career as a builder of Federal style wooden structures in the manner of Bulfinch (*see*) and Benjamin (*see*). After establishing himself in Boston he assumed the professional leadership left vacant by Bulfinch's de-

South View

10

parture, and, after contact with Bulfinch's late local designs, he became a leading exponent of the Boston granite style, that simple lithic Greco-Roman variation of neo-classicism that characterizes the local architectural scene from the teens onward. Among his major works were the Faneuil Hall Marketplace, 1823–1826, and the Stone Temple in Quincy, 1828. After 1827 he worked as an engineer and effectively ceased to practice architecture.

Parris drawings are not plentiful. They are scattered through a number of collections, including the American Antiquarian Society, the Boston Athenaeum, and the Bostonian Society.

REFERENCE: Edward F. Zimmer, *The Architectural Career of Alexander Parris*, Ann Arbor, 1985.

10. BOSTON ATHENAEUM, ca. 1823 (unbuilt project).

"South View" (exterior perspective) of a design presumably for the Boston Athenaeum, undated (watermark 1816). Signed: "Alexr Parris Architect No 93 Court St Boston." Graphite, ink, and wash on heavy (Whatman) paper, 19½ × 27¼". Boston Athenaeum.

During the 1820s the Athenaeum was seeking to expand its quarters. It moved from Tremont Street to Pearl Street in 1822, and Solomon Willard (*see*) designed an addition to its new building there in 1826. This is one of three related surviving drawings (the others are a first floor plan and an elevation) housed in the Athenaeum's archive. None is identified or dated, although two are on paper watermarked 1816. Parris's office was at 93 Court Street from 1818 through 1823. Presumably this archival perspective depicts a project for a new home of the mid-decade. The building would have been a rectangular three-story block capped by a shallow gable, with drafted masonry on the ground floor and smooth ashlar above. Windows are shown arcuated below, linteled above; the shallow pediment is enlivened with a wreathed bull's-eye; uncarved acroteria stand at the corners of the roof.

This is, apparently, the sole surviving perspective from Parris's hand and, again apparently, the earliest surviving perspective produced in Boston by someone other than Bulfinch (*see*). And, except for the application of even color washes (pale yellow for stone, grays for shade and voids), it shows little development over Bulfinch's 1788 drawing of the Hollis Street Church (Fig. 2). Both display a frontal elevation (parallel to the picture plane) and perpendicular planes receding to a vanishing point on one side. In Parris's drawing the latter is a pinhole in the left margin. Neither contains an indication of ambience, not even a horizon line in Parris's drawing, where the building "floats" untethered on the sheet. Neither Bulfinch nor Parris indicates sash, mullions, or transoms; each renders his windows as "blind."

Such similarities are explained by the fact that Parris still seems to work from the same eighteenth-century English authority as Bulfinch: Joshua Kirby's *Perspective of Architecture*, 1761. The older architect mentions Kirby specifically among other sources in his "Principles of Perspective"; although Kirby does not appear among the books Parris sold to the Athenaeum in 1826, he may have known the copy already in that library that bears an august provenance. It contains the pencil signature of "I Town 1806," and the ink inscription "Presented to the Boston Athenaeum by Mr Ashur [*sic*] Benjamin this 1 March 1810." Although Kirby explains perspective projection with buildings both parallel and at an angle to the picture plane, the bulk of his illustrations show the former. Plates LIX and LX, for instance, are outlined and shaded versions of a perspective of a building by Inigo Jones with one facade parallel to the picture plane (Fig. 4). It is probably coincidental that parallel belt courses, the upper one a continuous sill at the base of the second-story windows, appear in both Jones's and Parris's designs.

REFERENCES: Boston Athenaeum, *Continuity and Change. A Pictorial History of the Boston Athenaeum*, Boston, 1876, fig. 8 (incorrectly dated 1845); Boston Athenaeum, *A Climate for Art. The History of the Boston Athenaeum Gallery, 1827–1873*, Boston, 1980, 2–5; Zimmer, 445–446.

Ammi B. Young (1798–1874)

The career of Ammi Burnham Young, which stretched from New England to the federal capital, was centered, during its middle years, in the Boston area. Born in Lebanon, New Hampshire, he was trained by his father as a carpenter-builder but had assumed the titles of architect and civil engineer by 1830. His early work in Lebanon was largely in the Federal style. In 1830 he moved to Burlington, where he designed his first major monumental building, the Greek Doric Vermont State House of 1833–1836. The years 1837 to 1838 found him in Boston supervising his design for the federal customs house, a work that was a logical sequel to the Vermont State House if we recognize Young's contact with Alexander Parris (*see*) at this time. In 1852 he moved once again, to assume the office of supervising architect in the U.S. Treasury Department. Here his practice became prolific, national, and Italianate. He retired during the Civil War and died in Washington, D.C.

Young drawings exist in a number of collections including the National Archives in Washington, D.C.

REFERENCES: Osmund Overby, "Ammi B. Young, an Architectural Sketch," *Antiques*, 81, 1962, 530–533; Lawrence Wodehouse, "Ammi Burnham Young," *JSAH*, XXV, 1966, 268–280; Osmund Overby, "Young, Ammi B.," *MEA*, IV, 463–464.

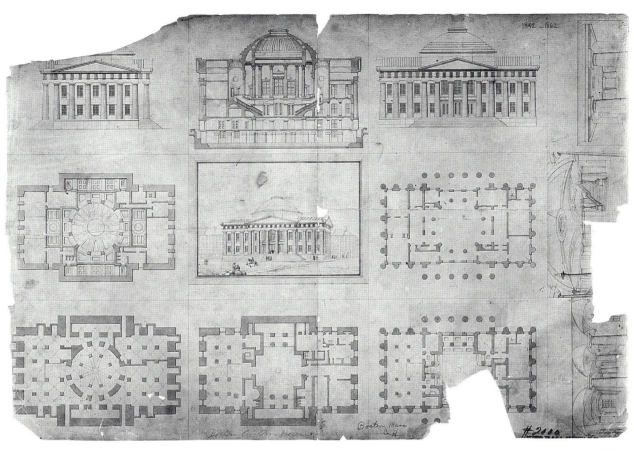

11

11. BOSTON CUSTOMS HOUSE, 1837–1847 (altered with addition of tower, 1911–1915).

Plans, elevations, section, and outline exterior and interior perspectives, undated. Unsigned. Black ink and gray wash on heavy paper, 23 × 34⅛″. National Archives, Washington, D.C.

The erection of a federal customs house in Boston, following the beginning of one in New York, was authorized in 1835. Ammi B. Young won the open competition for its design in 1837, besting projects by Richard Upjohn, Edward Shaw, Alexander Parris (*see*), Asher Benjamin (*see*), and others, and the building was slowly erected of Quincy granite over the next decade (it took three years to establish the foundations). The domed, cruciform, Greco-Roman monument was and is one of the major examples of the neo-classical phase of the Boston granite style, which was just then beginning to wane.

Probably sometime in 1837–1838 the architect engaged as his draftsman the young Hammatt Billings (*see*), apparently fresh from apprenticeships in illustration with Abel Bowen and in architecture with Asher Benjamin (thus abandoning a losing competitor for the winner). According to one of Billings's obituaries, written some thirty-five years after the event, "he did not design the building; but all the drawings were made by him. He was with Mr. Young three years." Such a sweeping claim for a young draftsman begs for contradiction, but if we exclude the surviving competition section published by Lowry, presumably made by Young before Billings arrived on the scene, we can probably give many of the remaining sheets to Billings. Hammatt won a diploma for drawings of the customs house exhibited in 1839 at the Massachusetts Charitable Mechanic Association in Boston. They may indeed have been, or included, this very sheet, which may plausibly be dated this same year.

Excluding the interior views on the right margin of the sheet, there are nine drawings, each occupying a separate rectangle. Notes mark for engraving the four upper rectangles to center and right containing longitudinal section, elevation, exterior perspective from the east (6 × 9″), and principal floor plan. There exists (at the Boston Athenaeum and elsewhere) an engraving entitled "NEW CUSTOM HOUSE, BOSTON. / A.B. YOUNG ARCHT.," which was entered by Young for copyright on 30 October 1840, with a copy deposited on 20 November of the same year. This (12³⁄₁₆ × 14½″ on a larger backing) depicts an exterior perspective from the east (4 × 6⅝″), plans of the principal and entrance floors, and a transverse section. The engraved exterior perspective, which follows that of the National Archives drawing in every respect save its shading and more plentiful staffage, was "Designed by C.H. Billings" and "Engraved by G.G. Smith." From this it can be suggested that Billings is the draftsman of the Archives drawing. Why that section marked for engraving on the drawing was not followed exactly in the engraving is unknown.

(There exists another, larger, outline, pencil perspective of the building from the east [8½ × 9¼″; mounted],

in the collection of the A.I.A., Washington, D.C. It is taken from the same viewpoint as the Archives perspective, but staffage and environment vary [the Old State House appears on the right, for instance]. This, too, may be given to Billings on the basis of the engraved view [5½ × 8⅛″ (image); Boston Athenaeum and elsewhere] of the CUSTOM-HOUSE, BOSTON, "Drawn by C.H. Billings," "Engraved by J. Archer," and "Published by S. Walker, Boston, 1843" which follows the format of this drawing in most details [again staffage is augmented and shading added].)

The format of this sheet may be given to Young on the basis of his drawing for the Vermont State House (Vermont Historical Society) in which an exterior perspective and three plans each occupy a quarter of a horizontally rectangular sheet, but here the draftsmanship is clearly Billings's, whose outline style (so different from the shaded exterior in Young's drawing) captures well the cool abstractness of the neo-classical design of the building. It follows the lead of such outline renderings of international neo-classicism as those that appear in publications by, for example, architects Friedrich Gilly, Friedrich Weinbrenner, or Percier and Fontaine, or of figurative illustrations by John Flaxman. As the building was under construction from presumably more detailed graphics when this sheet was drawn, this (or its engraved progeny) was probably intended for publicity.

Billings's published perspectives of the exterior of the customs house represent a major advance over Parris's perspective of his project for the Boston Athenaeum (Cat. 10) of the previ-

ous decade. They are fully rendered views set in typical ambiences, and probably reflect a variety of sources, including Young and A.J. Davis's recent Boston views.

REFERENCES: Library of Congress, Copyright Records, Massachusetts, vol. 57, 1840, 269; Lawrence Woodhouse, "Architectural Projects in the Greek Revival Style by Ammi Burnham Young," *Old-Time New England*, LX, January–March 1970, 73–85; Margaret Supplee Smith, "The Custom House Controversy," *Nineteenth Century*, III, 1977, 99–104; Bates Lowry, *Building a National Image*, Washington, D.C., 1985, 48–50, 214, and pl. 29; James F. O'Gorman, "H. and J.E. Billings of Boston," *JSAH*, XLII, March 1983, 55–56, notes 6–7, 12.

12. CHAPEL, MOUNT AUBURN CEMETERY, CAMBRIDGE, MASSACHUSETTS, 1843 (unbuilt competition entry).

Front elevation, undated. Unsigned. Ink and watercolor on heavy paper, 27⅞ × 28¼″. Society for the Preservation of New England Antiquities; gift of Dr. Wm. S. Bigelow, 1927.

Mount Auburn Cemetery was created in 1830–1831 by a group led by Jacob Bigelow, "one of the first theorists of American cemetery reform" (Linden-Ward). Several buildings in several styles were planned and erected for its picturesque layout. In 1832 Bigelow himself designed the Egyptian gateway that still marks the entrance. In 1843 a competition was held for the design of the nonsectarian chapel. The Society for the Preservation of New

12

England Antiquities has drawings by four contestants: Young, Bond (*see*), Bryant (*see*), and, presumably, Jacob Bigelow, whose project was built in 1845 (and rebuilt in 1858). It was described in the literature of the period as "a Westminster Abbey, Pantheon, or Valhalla, to contain statues, busts, and monuments of distinguished men."

This is one of a set of drawings submitted by Young for a chapel of cruciform plan with equal arms in perpendicular Gothic style. It shows a fully shaded elevation with just the slightest suggestion of ambience given by the ground line.

REFERENCES: Jacob Bigelow, *A History of the Cemetery of Mount Auburn*, Boston and Cambridge, 1860, 54 ff.; Blanche Linden-Ward, "Putting the Past in Place: The Making of Mount Auburn Cemetery," *Cambridge Historical Society Proceedings*, 44, 1976–1979 [1985], 171–192; Wodehouse, "Young," *JSAH*; Wodehouse, "Young," *Old-Time New England*.

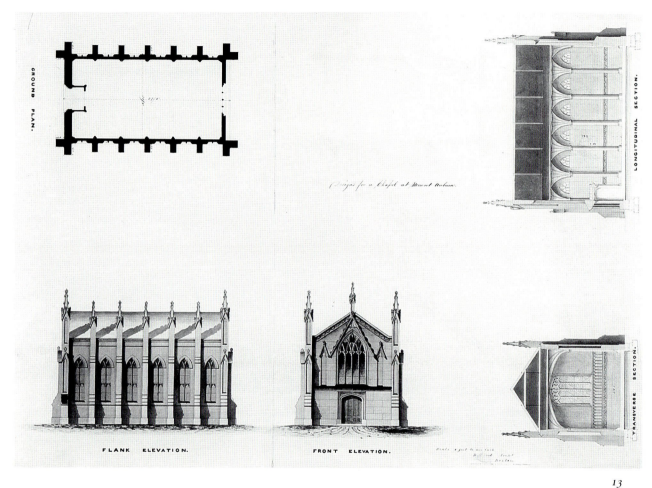

Designs for a Chapel at Mount Auburn

GROUND PLAN.

LONGITUDINAL SECTION.

TRANSVERSE SECTION.

FLANK ELEVATION.

FRONT ELEVATION.

13

Richard Bond
(1798–1861)

We know little about Bond's early years. He was practicing by 1826 when he designed the Green Street Church, and he worked in association with Isaiah Rogers at the First Parish Church, Cambridge, during 1833–1834. He began his own practice when Rogers moved to New York in the latter year. His City Hall, Salem, was erected 1837–1838. Bond designed Gore Hall (the library), 1838–1841, and the Lawrence Scientific School, 1847, for Harvard College. For Oberlin, Ohio, he provided drawings for the First Church, 1842–1844. He was associated with Charles E. Parker (*see*) from 1850 to 1853.

Richard Bond drawings are in scattered New England collections and in the Archives of Oberlin College, Ohio.

REFERENCES: E.F. Zimmer, *Alexander Parris*, 257–258; Goeffrey Blodgett, *Oberlin Architecture, College and Town*, Oberlin, 1985, 58–59.

13. CHAPEL, MOUNT AUBURN CEMETERY, CAMBRIDGE, MASSACHUSETTS, 1843 (unbuilt competition entry).

Plan, front and side elevations, and longitudinal and transverse sections of "Designs for a Chapel at Mount Auburn," undated. Signed: "R. Bond Archt / Boston." Ink and watercolor on heavy paper, 20½ × 27¾". Society for the Preservation of New England Antiquities; gift of Dr. Wm. S. Bigelow, 1927.

This is a small Gothic chapel project entered in the competition for Mount Auburn Cemetery (see Cat. 12). It is presented in simple, shaded orthographics with the slightest hint of ambience.

Isaiah Rogers
(1800–1869)

Rogers was born in Marshfield, Massachusetts, and apprenticed in 1817 to the Boston housewright Jese Shaw. In the early 1820s he practiced in Mobile, Alabama, then joined Solomon Willard (see). When Willard retired to the granite business in Quincy, Rogers took over his practice. Using Willard's stone he began a series of granite works, including the famed Greek Revival Tremont House in Boston, 1828–1829, designed when he was just 28. He was associated with Richard Bond (see) in 1834–1835, then moved on to New York to work on the Astor House while practicing in Richmond, Virginia, as well as locally. He designed the monumental Merchants Exchange in State Street, now demolished, in 1840. From 1848 he lived in Cincinnati, where, except for two years as architect of the U.S. Treasury during the Civil War, he practiced, after 1855 with his son, Solomon Willard Rogers, until his death.

Rogers drawings are not plentiful.

REFERENCES: Rogers's unpublished diaries are at the Avery Library, Columbia University; Denys Peter Myers, "Rogers, Isaiah," *MEA*, III, 599–602.

14. PRESIDENT'S HOUSE, HARVARD COLLEGE, CAMBRIDGE, MASSACHUSETTS, 1843–1846 (unbuilt project).

"Front Elevation," and partial diagrammatic section, undated. Unsigned. Graphite, ink, and washes on heavy (Whatman) paper (watermark 1845); 19½ × 27⅜". Harvard University Archives.

This unbuilt design falls between the fourth and fifth Harvard presidential residences, the latter erected in 1860 from designs of E.C. Cabot. On 1 December 1845, Rogers noted in his diary that "Mr. [Samuel Atkins] Eliot [Treasurer] called on me to see about making plan for a house for the President of Harvard College. Got Mr. Holmes to sign a receipt for one mislaid." He worked on the drawings over the following weeks, and showed the design to Eliot on the 17th. "He liked it very well," but suggested some changes, such as leaving off the piazza. On the 23rd Rogers notes more alterations requested by Edward Everett, Harvard president from 1846 to 1849. Work continued on the drawing through January of the next year, and plans, specifications, and an estimate were delivered on 14 February. Rogers records payment for $122.50 for his work on 3 March 1846, after which the project is unmentioned.

This is one of a set of designs and revisions and manuscript specifications for that residence preserved in Harvard Archives. One sheet, a plan of a variant design, has the inscription: "Boston Decr 8th 1843 / . . . I Rogers Archt." and may represent part of the "mislaid" set. There is another 1843 project for the Harvard President's House among the George M. Dexter (see) drawings at the Boston Athenaeum.

This is an orthographic projection isolated on the blank sheet with no indication of ambience but the merest suggestion of a penciled ground line. Within the confines of the building itself, however, the forms are fully rendered by smoothly washed shades and shadows which visually indicate the three-dimensional bulk of the semicircular central bay. They also firmly date this graphic to the first half of the century (see Cat. 25).

REFERENCES: Rogers's diary, Avery Library, Columbia University; Bainbridge Bunting (completed and edited by Margaret Henderson Floyd), *Harvard. An Architectural History*, Cambridge MA and London, 1985, 25, 289 note 5.

Front elevation

14

Jonathan Preston
(1801–1888)

Jonathan Preston's career exemplifies the changeover from builder to architect in the men of his generation. He was born in Beverly Farms and apprenticed around 1816 to a Boston mason. By 1824 he was in business for himself. Following a tradition established by Dawes, Bulfinch (*see*), and Sumner (*see*), he entered politics in the 1830s, serving as, among other positions, city councilman, 1838–41, and state legislator, 1845, 1849–50. Such public positions meant business for his office. Although "qualified" as an architect by 1830, he continued to use the title of mason until 1850, when he first listed himself as "Architect/ Builder." As he built for Isaiah Rogers (*see*) and E.C. Cabot, he may have been trained by either (he appropriated Rogers's Tremont House design for his own United States and Mt. Washington hotels in 1838). From 1857 to 1861 he practiced in partnership with W.R. Emerson, and from 1862 with his son, William G. (*see*). He "retired" around 1875, but was officially part of the Preston firm until his death.

The collection of drawings from the Preston firm (father and son), now owned by the Boston Public Library, constitutes one of the most complete sets of architectural graphics preserved from the nineteenth century.

REFERENCE: Jean Ames Follett-Thompson, "The Business of Architecture: William Gibbons Preston and Architectural Professionalism in Boston during the Second Half of the Nineteenth Century," Ph.D. diss., Boston University, 1986, chapter II.

15. CHAPEL, HARVARD COLLEGE, CAMBRIDGE, MASSACHUSETTS, 1855 (unbuilt competition entry).

15a. "Plan," undated. Unsigned. Ink and lavender wash on heavy paper, 21¼ × 15½". Harvard University Archives.

15b. "End Elevation," undated. Unsigned. Graphite, red ink, and gray wash with graphite emendations on heavy paper, 15½ × 21¼". Harvard University Archives.

The finished drawing shows no tower or other vertical accent, but there is a faintly penciled bellcote over the ridge and a faintly penciled study of a pinnacle to the right.

15c. "Lateral Section Showing Orchestral Gallery" and "Lateral Section Showing Chancel," undated. Unsigned. Graphite, ink, and pink, gray, and blue washes on heavy paper, 15½ × 21¼". Harvard University Archives.

Harvard held a competition for the design of its chapel in 1855, a competition won by Paul Schulze. Projects by other entrants are preserved at the Archives (E.C. Cabot and Arthur Gilman [*see*]) and at the Avery Library, Columbia University (Richard Upjohn).

These are numbers 1, 2, and 4 of a set of five sheets identified on the archival folder as "Jonathan Preston / Proposed Design for a Chapel 1855." The archival attribution can be taken as accurate. Jean Follett has recognized the same hand in some drawings for the Boston Society of Natural History building (*see*) and the Massachusetts Institute of Technology, both by Jonathan and his son, William (*see*). These naive graphics have been aptly characterized in correspondence by Follett as "painfully compass-drawn." They are thoroughly conventional and certainly the work of a self-taught draftsman with a firm grip on the ruling pen. As with other sheets of the time, rendered orthographics float on the white paper unlocated as to ambience. Their distinguishing feature is the draftsman's unusual sense of color.

REFERENCES: Bainbridge Bunting (completed and edited by Margaret Henderson Floyd), *Harvard. An Architectural History*, Cambridge MA and London, 1985, 46 and 291 note 23; Jean Follett to author, 11 February 1988.

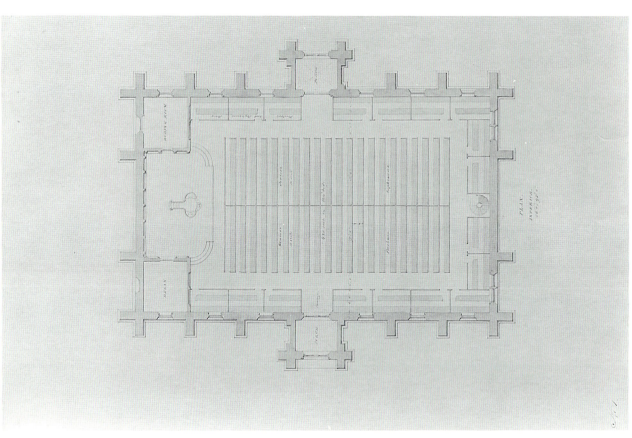

15a

END ELEVATION.

15b

LATERAL SECTION showing ORCHESTRAL GALLERY.

LATERAL SECTION SHOWING CHANCEL.

15c (see also plate 3)

Charles G. Hall
(active locally during the second quarter of the nineteenth century)

Hall first appears in the Boston directories in 1825 and continues to be listed to 1846. In 1827 he may have been associated with Alexander Parris (*see*), and, as this drawing shows, he had some connection to G.M. Dexter (*see*), if only in shared office space.

REFERENCE: Edward F. Zimmer, *The Architectural Career of Alexander Parris*, Ann Arbor, 1985, 256–257, 542–543.

16. HOUSE, PHILLIPS PLACE, BOSTON, 1836.

Plan, elevation, sections, full-size profiles, and specification notes for a "Doorway for Houses on East side of Phillips Place / . . . August 1836." "Drawn [by] . . . / C.G. Hall. / Office corner of Court and Tremont Sts. / Boston." Black ink and watercolors with graphite notes on heavy (Whatman) paper (watermark 1835), 26½ × 19″. Boston Athenaeum.

This sheet, one of a set, details a granite, Greek Revival doorway set into a brick townhouse off Stoughton Street in Dorchester. It is one of a series of designs signed by Hall as architect found in this volume of the Dexter drawings. This is an early example of the detailed graphic directions that will grow in number over the course of the century.

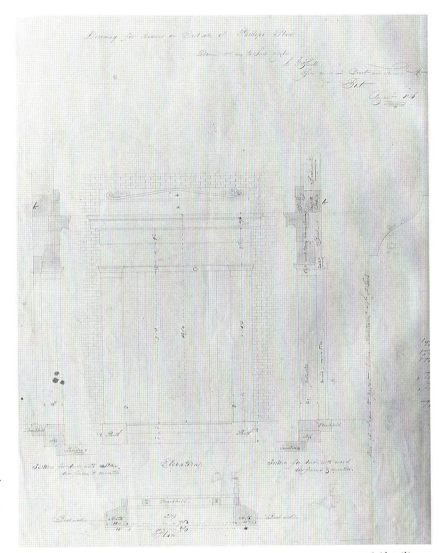

16 (detail)

George M. Dexter (1802–1872)

George Minot Dexter was born in Boston and educated at Harvard University. Influenced on his European travels during the 1820s by the work of the German neo-classicists, Dexter on his return in 1831 was trained in engineering by Loammi Baldwin and in architecture by Alexander Parris (*see*). Dexter practiced in Boston from 1836 until 1852, when he became president of the Vermont and Canada Railroad. His clientele ranged from the early railroads to commercial interests to domestic builders, and he planned suburban Longwood in Brookline. He was a founding member of the American Society of Civil Engineers and became its president in 1850. After 1852 his practice was assumed by N.J. Bradlee (*see*). There is a memorial to his memory in Trinity Church, Copley Square.

Dexter's graphic remains fill eleven volumes containing more than 1,200 drawings; they are now owned by the Boston Athenaeum. Together with the many volumes of Bradlee drawings in the same collection, they reflect the continuous production of sequential architectural firms for nearly a half century, beginning in the mid-1830s, and, with the 55 volumes of William Preston (*see*) drawings ranging from 1861 to 1907 in the Boston Public Library, the volumes of drawings by George F. Fuller in the Avery Library, Columbia University, and the H.H. Richardson (*see*) collection at the Houghton Library of Harvard University, they form an unparalleled graphic lode for one nineteenth-century American city.

REFERENCES: Jonathan Pearlman, "Dexter, George Minot," *MEA*, I, 570; Jonathan Pearlman, "Dexter, George Minot," in William H. Jordy and Christopher P. Monkhouse, *Buildings on Paper: Rhode Island Architectural Drawings 1825–1945*, Providence, 1982, 213.

17. O. GOODWIN STORE BUILDING, WASHINGTON STREET, BOSTON, undated.

"Third Story floor" and "Garret floor" framing plans plus details of roof trusses, undated. Unsigned. Black ink and watercolors on heavy (Whatman) paper, 26½ × 18¹¹⁄₁₆". Boston Athenaeum.

The Goodwin Store was a traditional wood-span, load-bearing masonry structure.

This is one of an "Office copy" set. Although it is clearly a working drawing, or sheet of detailed directions for the builder, it is as clearly too visually attractive to be abused at the building site. The bound volumes of drawings left by Dexter, Bradlee (*see*), and George Fuller must represent continuous office records from which working drawings were produced. Such compilations certainly allowed for easy office reference when questions arose at the site. Before the era of photo-reproduction, copies for use on the job (or for subsequent jobs) were made from sheets such as this (*see* Cat. 20). Since the heavy Whatman paper was not transparent, such a sheet (though not this one) often has pinholes left by the duplicating process know as "pouncing."

18. D.S. GREENOUGH'S STORE, WASHINGTON AND SCHOOL STREETS, BOSTON, 1843.

"Front Elevation on Washington Street" and "Transverse Section," "Boston, April 26th 1843." Unsigned. Black ink with gray wash and watercolors with graphite notes and additions on heavy (Whatman) paper, 19 × 26½". Boston Athenaeum.

D.S. Greenough is listed as a counselor with offices at 23 Court Street in the *Boston Directory* for 1843. He apparently never worked at this address and must have built the store as an investment, or he represented an unnamed client.

The hammered stone front is a commercial example of the Boston granite style. The heavy timber construction (including "fire-cut" beams shown in section) follows technology established for the New England mill, with the addition of iron columns behind the ground floor (plate?) glazing and at the second and third levels. Such a hybrid structural system may be characteristic of local building during mid-century.

This is one of a set of drawings for this store. It is characteristic of Dexter's graphics in general and those of his contemporaries. Inked orthogonals are enlivened with even washes of color used diagrammatically to indicate materials; three-dimensional projections, whether of whole buildings or structural details, are rare in this era (but not unknown; *see* Cats. 19, 22).

19. DEXTER-HALL HOUSE, COTTAGE FARM, BROOKLINE, MASSACHUSETTS, 1850–1851.

Exterior perspective, undated. Unsigned. Black ink and gray washes on

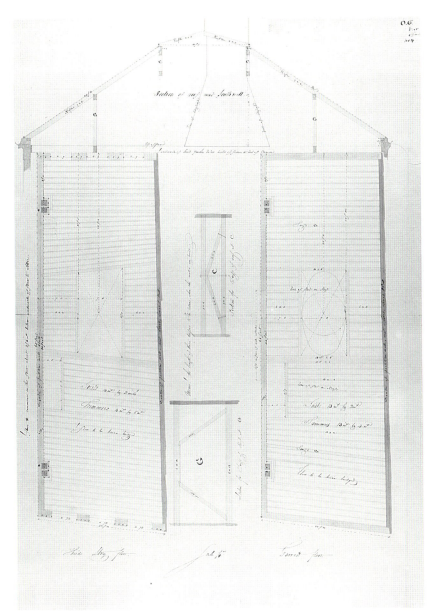

17

heavy (Whatman) paper, 9¼ × 12¾″ image on 13 × 18¾″ sheet. Boston Athenaeum.

Volume 11 of the Dexter drawings contains sets of sheets for the main house, the stable, and the "small house" at the Amos A. Lawrence Estate at Cottage Farm, like Longwood (*see* Cat. 30) a suburban, residential Brookline community developed in the middle of the century. Dexter designed many houses in the area. The architect himself acquired property from Lawrence in 1850 and erected this cruciform, stone, Tudor cottage (now 156 Ivy Street) the next year.

This is the only perspective rendering in all the Dexter volumes. The simplified block of the building is shown in two-point projection with shades and shadows and some suggestion of wispy clouds in the sky, but no ambience. Except for its double vanishing points, which descend from Kirby's *Perspective*, this stark, block-on-table-plane image is visually little advanced over Parris's project for the Athenaeum of a generation earlier (Cat. 10).

REFERENCES: Pauline Chase Harrell and Margaret Supplee Smith, eds., *Victorian Boston Today*, Boston, 1975, 56–68; Brookline Historical Commission.

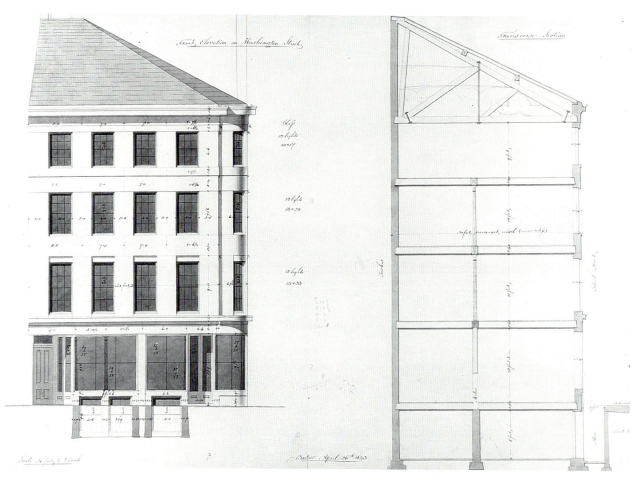

19 (see also plate 4)

Nathaniel J. Bradlee
(1829–1888)

Born in Boston and educated at Chauncy Hall School, Nathaniel Jeremiah Bradlee learned his profession in apprenticeship from 1845 to 1852 with George M. Dexter (*see*), to whose practice he succeeded. For the next 35 years he worked as a solid professional, becoming a founding member of the Boston Society of Architects and turning out numerous private, public, ecclesiastical, railroad, and other commissions in a succession of styles fashionable at the time, from the Gothic and Italianate of his early days to the Second Empire and Victorian Gothic of the post–Civil War years. In 1872 he made Walter T. Winslow (1843–1909) his partner, and in 1884 he added George Homans Wetherell to the firm. He retired in 1886, but the office of Bradlee, Winslow & Wetherell continued to operate.

Bradlee's graphic remains encompass 32 volumes containing an estimated 5,620 individual drawings, now housed in the Boston Athenaeum. This must be one of the most complete graphic records of a mid-nineteenth-century architectural practice (especially when joined to the 11 volumes of surviving drawings from the predecessor firm of Dexter), and, when added to the nine volumes left by George F. Fuller (in the Avery Library, Columbia University) and 55 volumes of drawings from the firm of William G. Preston (*see*), and the H.H. Richardson (*see*) collection at the Houghton Library of Harvard University, form an extraordinary local graphic record. Not only do these volumes record in detail the course of Bradlee's career, but they form an im-

portant source for the study of the development of architectural graphics in the last century. One can, for example, witness the gradual introduction just before 1870 of tracing paper (especially at first for framing diagrams) as a supplement to the standard, heavy Whatman Turkey Mill papers previously used by everyone (an introduction paralleled in the Preston remains). According to A.O. Halse, tracing paper "was first manufactured as a definite commodity for professional use in 1862," and tracing cloth or linen dates from the same period. This was certainly occasioned by developments in photo-reproductive methods resulting in the use of the blueprinting process as an easier means of copying drawings for field use than the old methods of tracing required by opaque paper. The process was described by the British astronomer and chemist John Frederick William Herschel in the 1840s, but only slowly did it change drafting room practice. As late as 1878 a note in *AABN* described, in a voice that suggests the novelty of the subject, how an office boy might make a blueprint using sunlight.

REFERENCES: "The 'Blue' Copying Process," *AABN*, IV, 3 August 1878, 44; A.O. Halse, "A History of the Developments in Architectural Drafting Techniques," D.Ed. diss., New York University, 1952, 402 ff.; Karen A. Guffey, "The Architectural Drawings of Nathaniel J. Bradlee," Boston Athenaeum, 1984.

20. STORE FOR EDWARD BANGS, WASHINGTON STREET, BOSTON, 1854.

"Front Elevaton of Iron Truss" plus details, "Sept 1854." Signed: "Nathl J.

Bradlee Archt Boston." Black and red inks and watercolor washes on heavy (Whatman) paper, 27 × 18⅝". Boston Athenaeum.

Bradlee's "Iron Truss" is a hybrid. It combines cast-iron imposts and "keystone" and iron tension ties with brick arch segments in compression in a curious mixture of the traditional and the industrial, which, at this date, suggests a timidity with which local designers introduced new materials and methods. Castings and assembly are minutely prescribed.

This is one of a large set of drawings for this store. As with other drawings preserved from Bradlee's practice, it is clearly a working drawing which has never left the office. Although this does not exhibit pouncing holes, it was copied. Pages 208–209 of volume 3 contain a black-ink outline version of this sheet of details intended for another structure, a store for John Collamore, Jr., at 190 Washington Street, dated 1855.

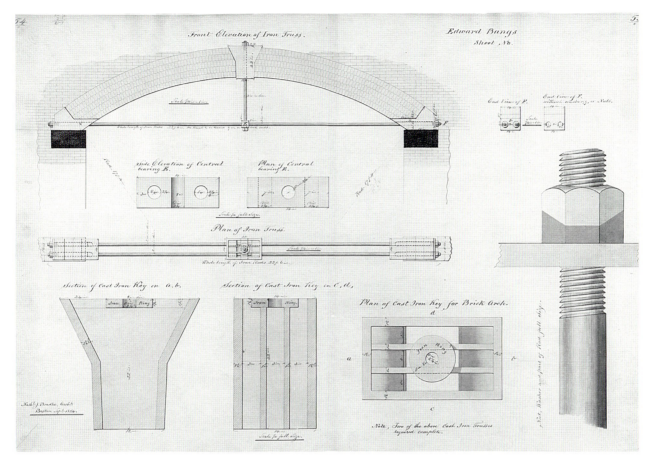

Front Elevation of Iron Truss.

Edward Bangs
Sheet No.

End View of F.
End View of F.
without washing, or Nuts.

Side Elevation of Central
bearing B.

Plan of Central
bearing B.

Plan of Iron Truss.

Section of Cast Iron Key on A, b.

Section of Cast Iron Key on C, d.

Plan of Cast Iron Key for Brick Arch.

Note. Two of the above Cast Iron Trusses
required complete.

20

21. C.G. LORING AND COMPANY STORE, CONGRESS STREET, BOSTON, 1855.

Diagrammatic "Front Elevation," "June 9th 1855." Signed: "Nathl Bradlee Archt." Red, blue, and black ink and graphite on heavy paper embossed with architect's oval stamp, 19 × 27″. The Boston Athenaeum.

This commercial block for a window glass concern was another technological hybrid: on the exterior, a granite building with cast-iron shopfront; on the interior, a structure of iron posts and wooden beams.

The drawing, one of a large set for Caleb Loring's store, contains quarryman's and glazier's figures: each granite block (above the metalic shopfront) is dimensioned in red, each pane of glass dimensioned in blue. Again, this is undoubtedly the office record, copies of which went out to the trades.

REFERENCE: Guffey, "Bradlee," 9.

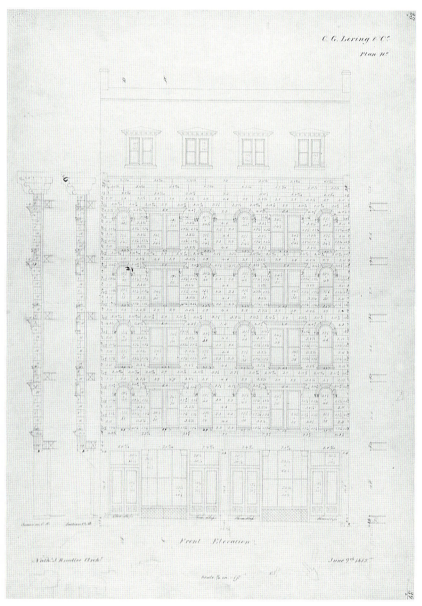

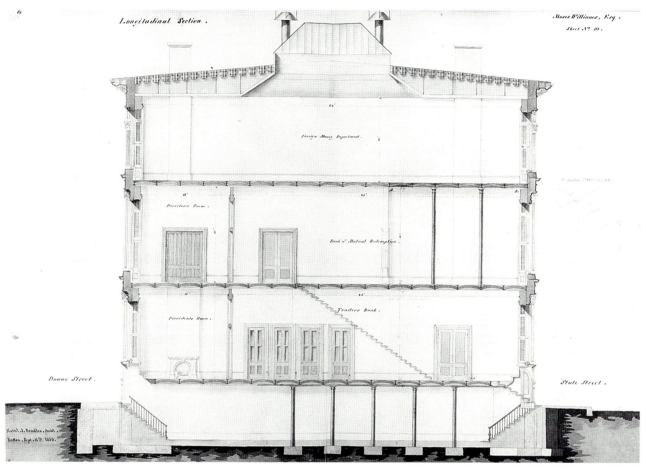

22 (see also plate 5)

22. BANK BUILDING FOR MOSES WILLIAMS, BETWEEN DOANE AND STATE STREETS, BOSTON, 1858.

"Longitudinal Section" plus an isometric structural detail ("Construction of Floor"), "Sept. 11th 1858." Signed: "Natl J. Bradlee, Archt / Boston." Black ink and watercolors with graphite notes on heavy (Whatman) paper, 19 × 27⅛". Boston Athenaeum.

Moses Williams was a principal in J.D. & M. Williams, wine merchants, at 185–187 State Street, according to the *Boston Directory* of 1858. Perhaps he commissioned this block as an investment.

This is one of an office set of signed contract documents. The construction is of cast-iron beams and columns with brick floor arches and a timber frame roof. The fronts are also of cast iron. Such an iron structure was ap-

parently rare enough in Boston to call forth an isometric detail unusual in Bradlee's graphic remains (or, for that matter, mid-nineteenth-century Boston in general), although iron construction such as this was common in New York by this date.

This is an analytical section of great clarity achieved by color coding materials. This was increasingly necessary because of the technological developments since Bulfinch's time.

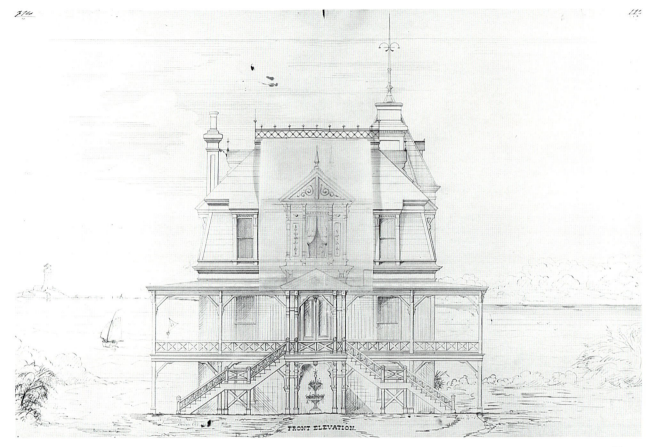

FRONT ELEVATION.

23. HASKELL SEASIDE
COTTAGE, 1871.

"Front Elevation," "Oct 1871."
Signed: "N.J. Bradlee. Archt. / Boston." Black ink on heavy paper with
graphite additions, and a graphite
sketch enlarging and altering the central dormer on affixed tracing paper
flap, 18¼ × 26½". Boston
Athenaeum.

This shows a project for an unlocated,
three-and-a-half-story, stick style,
mansarded cottage with surrounding,
two-story gallery for a client identified only by surname. The drawing
shows an orthographic projection in
stiffly ruled ink lines set into a free-
hand ink line landscape setting. Its
tight draftsmanship should be compared with William Preston's fluid
Baldwin house drawing of two decades later (Cat. 46).

Gridley J.F. Bryant (1816–1899)

The son of an engineer and granite contractor, Gridley James Fox Bryant was trained by Loammi Baldwin and Alexander Parris (*see*). He was on his own by 1837, beginning a long career which saw him develop the largest architectural office in Boston. From this office came a vast number of buildings erected all over New England, many in the Boston granite style with which Bryant's name is closely connected. Major local works include the Suffolk County Jail, 1848–1851, the old City Hall (with Arthur Gilman [*see*]), 1860–1865, and a host of granite commercial buildings in the downtown section both before and after the fire of 1872. Bryant seems to have been primarily an organization man, and he used a succession of casual designers and partners over his long career, including Hammatt Billings (*see*), Gilman, and Louis P. Rogers.

Bryant's drawings are scattered over public and private collections; new ones come to light every year.

REFERENCES: "A Complete Catalogue of Plans, Specifications, Architectural Drawings, Photographs, Etc., the Property of Gridley J.F. Bryant, Esq., Architect, 28 State St., Boston, in Custody of Henry J. Bailey, North Situate, Mass., 1890," manuscript in the library of the University of Oregon; Henry T. Bailey, "An Architect of the Old School," *New England Magazine*, 25, 1901, 326–348; Robert B. MacKay, "Bryant, Gridley J.F.," *MEA*, I, 316–317; James F. O'Gorman, "Two Granite Tents at Bay View on Cape Ann," *Essex Institute Historical Collections*, 118, October 1982, 241–247.

24. CHAPEL, MOUNT AUBURN CEMETERY, CAMBRIDGE, MASSACHUSETTS, 1843 (unbuilt competition entry).

Analytical "Tranverse Section through Transepts" and rendered "Front Elevation" of a "Chapel, Mount Auburn Cemetery," "Boston, November 1st, 1843." Signed: "G.J.F. Bryant" (beneath tab now partially removed). Ink and watercolor on heavy paper, 27¼ × 19⅛". Society for the Preservation of New England Antiquities; gift of the estate of Wm. S. Bigelow, 1927.

This Gothic project, entered in the competition for the design of the cemetery chapel, is in a style unusual in Bryant's work but dictated by the character of the edifice (*see* Cat. 12).

The shaded elevation is flanked and partially obscured by rendered deciduous trees, a depiction of ambient nature not previously seen in this collection (other than Cat. 11), even in perspectives. By the 1840s the relationship between a building, especially a Gothic building, and its natural environment was a central concern to theoreticians like A.J. Downing and architects like A.J. Davis.

25. UNIVERSITY ("AGASSIZ") MUSEUM, HARVARD UNIVERSITY, CAMBRIDGE, MASSACHUSETTS, ca. 1860 (unbuilt project).

"Principal Entrance Facade" of the "Agassiz Museum," undated. Signed: "Gridley J.F. Bryant, Archt." Watercolor on heavy paper, 17½ × 25" (sight). Society for the Preservation of New England Antiquities.

The University Museum was the idea of Louis Agassiz; it grew unit by unit

from 1859 to 1913, beginning with the initial design by Henry Greenough and George Snell, whose contract drawings are in Harvard Archives. Also in Archives is a set signed by Bryant, including plans and elevations, which seem to be measured drawings of the Greenough-Snell building (or copies of their drawings), plus an outline side elevation of the design shown in this rendered elevation. None of this set is dated, nor does any sheet contain a watermark. All that can be said definitely about the date of Bryant's work is that it must stem from the period between the original construction and the first addition, also by Greenough and Snell, in 1871.

A project by Bryant is not mentioned by Bunting and Floyd. This Italianate design fits nicely a date around 1860, so we must assume it to be an alternative to the simple brick building erected, or, more likely, since Bryant's drawings other than his own facades show a building identical to the Greenough-Snell design, a remodeling of it. Could this be a project to dress up the principal facade of the Greenough-Snell building? The horizontal and vertical number and grouping of windows are identical in the drawing and the building.

Here Bryant (or, perhaps more likely, his draftsman) shows the museum in an orthographic projection the richness of whose washes and shadows contrasts sharply with its isolated setting upon the otherwise blank paper (so unlike the earlier elevation of the Mount Auburn chapel, Cat. 24). No ambience is indicated; even the ground line is weak. The handling of the washes is much looser than those in Isaiah Rogers's elevation of the President's House (Cat. 14), which is otherwise graphically related to this drawing, and that difference as well as the differences in style between the projected buildings measure the changes that took place in the development of architecture and drafting between the 1840s and the years around and after 1860.

REFERENCE: Bainbridge Bunting (completed and edited by Margaret Henderson Floyd), *Harvard. An Architectural History*, Cambridge MA, 1985, 93–96.

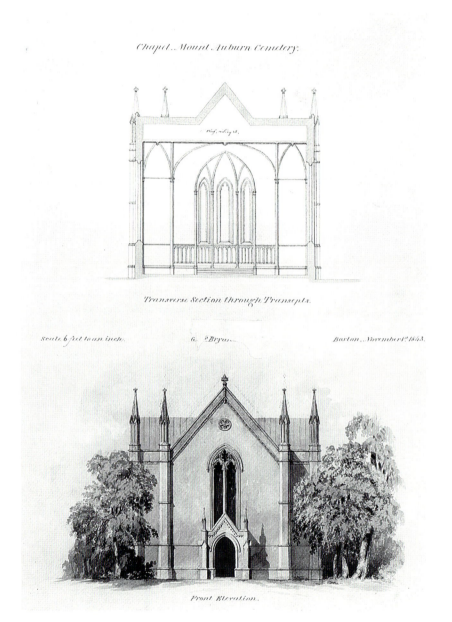

Chapel, Mount Auburn Cemetery.

Transverse Section through Transepts.

Scale 6 feet to an inch.   G. ? Bryant   Boston, November 1st 1843.

Front Elevation.

24

Agassiz Museum.

CITY HALL, BOSTON, MASS.
Gridley J.F. Bryant & Arthur Gilman, Architects.   Joseph M. Wightman, Mayor.

26

26. CITY HALL, BOSTON,
1860–1865 (interior remodeled).

Exterior perspective of "City Hall, Boston, Mass.," undated. Signed: "C Fehmer del." "Gridley J.F. Bryant & Arthur Gilman, Architects" (on mount). "Joseph M Wightman, Mayor" (on mount). Ruled ink and gray wash on heavy paper, 18¾ × 25¼". Private Collection.

Before 1860 city government was centered in Bulfinch's old Suffolk County Court House, 1810–1812, which had been remodeled in 1840 by Bryant as Boston's first city hall. On 18 February 1860 the City Council appointed a sub-committee to oversee the enlargement of that building. Six architects were invited to present plans: E.C. Cabot, N.J. Bradlee (*see*), S.S. Woodcock, J.R. Richards, W.R. Emerson, and G.J.F. Bryant. Only the last four submitted designs, although a fifth plan was subsequently received from H. Billings (*see*). Bryant won the competition with a Second Empire design, but nothing was done until 1862 (with Wightman as mayor) when Bryant, in partnership with Gilman, was asked to produce a building which would not extend but replace the old remodeled court house. The former structure was pulled down in 1863 and the new building, perhaps the first Second Empire building erected in America, was dedicated in 1865. These facts suggest the date 1862 for this drawing.

This may be the earliest document of immigrant Carl Fehmer's (*see*) professional presence. The 24-year-old delineator here turns out a sophisticated gray wash drawing that is almost photographic in its precision. As a presentation perspective it is a vast improvement on Dexter's drawing of a mere dozen years earlier (Cat. 19).

REFERENCES: *Report of the Committee on Public Buildings upon an Enlargement of the City Hall in a Southerly Direction* (City Document No. 44), Boston, 1860; George L. Wrenn III, "The Boston City Hall," *JSAH*, XXI, March 1962, 188–192; Harold Kirker, *The Architecture of Charles Bulfinch*, Cambridge MA, 1969, 263.

27. BEEBE AND BREWER RESIDENCES, 29 AND 30 BEACON STREET, BOSTON, 1864 (demolished 1917).

Presentation elevation of "Town residences of James M. Beebe & Gardner Brewer / covering the John Hancock estate on / Beacon Street, Boston, Mass." (on mount), undated. "G.J.F. Bryant, Archt." (on mount). Ruled graphite, ink, and sepia wash on heavy paper, $11\frac{1}{2} \times 14\frac{7}{8}$". Private Collection.

The Thomas (John) Hancock House (1736) on Beacon Hill was the subject of one of the first battles waged over historic preservation. It was pulled down in 1863. The site was immediately occupied by this pair of townhouses designed by Bryant's office (according to the credit on this drawing, without Arthur Gilman, who was nominally Bryant's partner at the time. They were associated on City Hall [Cat. 26], still under construction, but Gilman had also been sympathetic to the preservation of the demolished landmark. Perhaps he wished to have no part in its replacement). The French Second Empire exterior covered Eastlakian interiors (at least at No. 30 [Beebe's]) until these too were removed to make way for the extention of the State House.

This unsigned presentation elevation, with cast shadows and suggestions of ambience, shows the twin, reverse-plan houses precisely as built. It shares graphic characteristics with Fehmer's perspective of City Hall and may also have been executed by him.

REFERENCES: Arthur Gilman, "The Hancock House and its Founder," *Atlantic Monthly*, XI, 1863, 692–707; Margaret Henderson Floyd, "Measured Drawings of the Hancock House by John Hubbard Sturgis," in A.L. Cummings, ed., *Architecture in Colonial Massachusetts*, Boston, 1979, 87–111; Jane Holtz Kay, *Lost Boston*, Boston, 1980, 117.

Town residences of James M. Beebe & Gardner Brewer
erecting the John Hancock estate on
Beacon Street, Boston, Mass.
G.J.F. Bryant, Arch't.

Charles Roath
(active locally from 1830 to 1849)

Roath made the leap from mechanic to designer almost overnight. From 1830 to 1834 he is listed in the Boston directories as a stair builder; in 1835 he changed that to architect and presumably never looked back. His drafting room was at 23 Joy's Building during the 1840s.

28. TOWNHOUSES AND STORE, 1846.

28a. Plans of house with shop front, "Oct 21st 1846." Signed: "Charles Roath." Ink and watercolor with graphite emendations on heavy (Whatman) paper (watermarked 1846), 19½ × 13½". Society for the Preservation of New England Antiquities.

28b. Elevation and front wall sections of adjacent houses, one with shop front, "Oct 21st 1846." Signed: "Charles Roath." Ink and watercolor on heavy (Whatman) paper, 19½ × 13½". Society for the Preservation of New England Antiquities.

These are two of five preserved sheets devoted to a pair of unidentified and unlocated townhouses of brick with the one to the right incorporating a characteristic Boston style granite pier and lintel storefront at ground level. The brick load-bearing walls and wooden spans are otherwise traditional, and they required relatively minimal graphics beyond the arrangement of rooms and facade details.

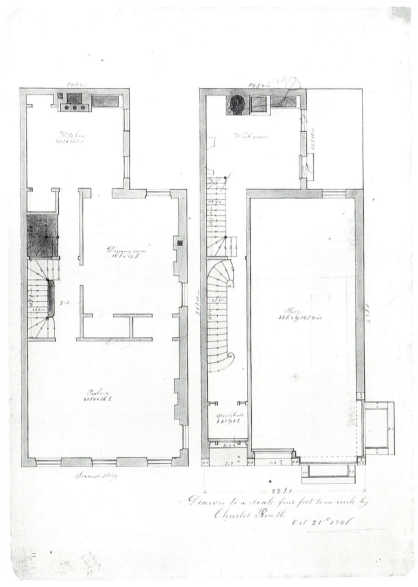

28a

20 f.   22 f.

Drawn to a scale four feet to an inch by
Charles Routh
Oct 21st 1846

28b

29

S. Charles Bugbee (active in Boston 1846–1861)

Samuel Charles Bugbee is listed as an architect in the Boston directories from 1846 through 1861, after which he is said to have moved to San Francisco.

29. PAVILION HOTEL, GLOUCESTER, MASSACHU-SETTS, 1849 (destroyed by fire, 1914).

"End Elevation" and "Front Elevation of Mason House," undated. Unsigned. Ink and watercolor with graphite notes on heavy paper, 19 × 26″. Cape Ann Historical Association; gift of Mrs. Julian James.

The railroad was laid out along the North Shore in the 1840s, and the Pavilion was Gloucester's first resort hotel, or, to quote the late local chronicler, Alfred Brooks, the fishing town's "first conspicuous monument of the profitable and ever-increasing business of housing and feeding the

summer people." It was erected between April and June of 1849 on a prominent waterfront site at the northern end of the axis of Gloucester harbor. Surrounded by "a rare variety of wood, water, head land, hill, bay and ocean," it offered swimming at its doorstep and relaxation on two-storied galleries swept by "healthy and invigorating sea breezes," according to contemporary advertising. The building figures conspicuously in *Gloucester Harbor* (1852) and other paintings and drawings by the port's resident luminist, Fitz Hugh Lane.

The owner was Sidney Mason (1799–1871); the architect, according to the Boston *Daily Evening Transcript* of 29 June 1849, was Charles Bugbee. Surely his double-tiered pavilion derives from the Nahant Hotel, erected 1822–1823, and other galleried, seaside hostelries that dotted the North Shore in the early nineteenth century, although it may ultimately stem from sources in the Caribbean where Mason spent some years.

Two sheets survive for the building. One contains a pair of preliminary plans showing a long, rectangular block surrounded by a piazza at each level, with public rooms on the first floor and guest rooms above reached by a sweeping stair in the central hall. This sheet of preliminary elevations, rendered in ruled ink lines and even, delicate washes, shows a two-and-a-half-story wooden structure with gable roof (whose multiple small dormers indicate another row of guest rooms at this level) and central bracketed cupola giving light to the stairhall below. Lane's views, and those of old photographs, indicate the alterations made during further study or construction: the bracketed lower piazza became a light wooden arcade, the central dormer was split in two, and the bracketed cupola was enlarged and simplified.

These orthographic projections, enlivened by cast shadows, consistent washes, and the barest suggestion of ambience, are characteristic of routine mid-century architectural graphics.

REFERENCES: "The Pavilion that Sidney Built," in James F. O'Gorman, *This Other Gloucester*, Boston, 1976, 30–37; John Wilmerding *et al.*, *Paintings by Fitz Hugh Lane*, Washington, D.C., and New York, 1988, 28.

Arthur D. Gilman
(1821–1882)

With the appearance of Arthur Delavan Gilman, the architectural profession in Boston began to include educated designers and theorists who had never worked at a building trade. A degree from Harvard or other institute of higher learning, or time spent abroad at the Ecole des Beaux-Arts or in traveling, replaced older, practical preparation.

Born at Newburyport, Massachusetts, Gilman was educated at Trinity College, Hartford (Class of 1840), and then in Europe. Returning to Boston, he established his presence as a lecturer and writer who especially championed the Renaissance Revival style exemplified by the work of Charles Barry in London. He established an office in Boston in 1845, immediately designing the Gothic Winter Street Church in Bath, Maine. He worked with E.C. Cabot until 1857, designed the Arlington Street Church, 1859–1861, and from 1859 until 1867 formed a firm with G.J.F. Bryant (*see*). After 1867 he joined Edward H. Kendall in a New York office.

Gilman drawings are rare, which makes the extraordinary set of detailed sheets for the Winter Street Church in the Maine Maritime Museum, Bath, all the more important.

REFERENCE: Margaret Henderson Floyd, "Gilman, Arthur Delavan," *MEA*, II, 208–210.

30. RESIDENCE, LONGWOOD, BROOKLINE, MASSACHUSETTS, 1858–1860.

30a. "Plan of First Floor," "Boston, July 1858." Signed: "Arthur Gilman Archt." Ink and wash on heavy (Whatman) paper (watermark 1856), 14¾ × 18⅞". Society for the Preservation of New England Antiquities.

30b. "Front Elevation & [partial] Section," "Boston July 1858." Signed: "Arthur Gilman Archt." Note upper right: "Plans No. 1 to 12 inclusive refered to in a contract made between us dated May 26 1860 W S Robinson D Sears Jr by C U Cotting Plan No 1 CUC." Ink and wash on heavy (Whatman) paper (watermark 1858), 14¾ × 18⅞". Society for the Preservation of New England Antiquities.

A note in the folder containing this set of drawings identifies this as the residence of Joseph Hall Cotton in Longwood, and these may be drawings for the house (now demolished) erected on Chatham Street (corner Kent) facing Longwood Park (now Square). The Longwood location is suggested by the names on the elevational sheet. David Sears began to develop this suburban area in the eastern end of Brookline in the early 1820s; in 1848 he divided it between his children. Charles U. Cotting was his friend and business associate. By 1855, when *Ballou's Pictorial* described the area as a "beautiful tract . . . [with] many fine hedges, lawns, and opening vistas, commanding beautiful views," a railroad station had been built. Residential design in the area consisted largely of two styles, the Downing picturesque and the French mansard, of which Gilman's four-square, two-and-

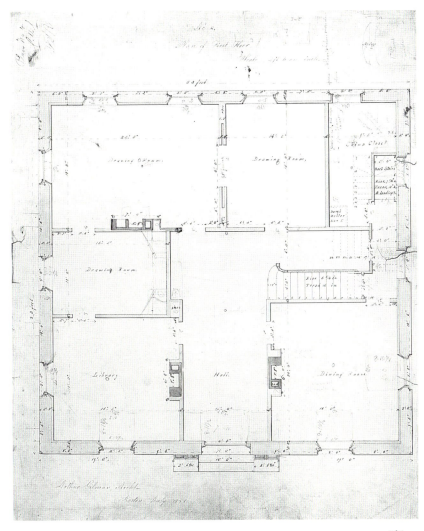

30a

a-half-story design is an example.

Gilman's orthographic plan and elevation presentation represents, unchanged from the eighteenth century, the essential graphics of architectural design.

REFERENCES: Pauline Chase Harrell and Margaret Supplee Smith, *Victorian Boston Today. Ten Walking Tours*, Boston, 1975, 56–69; Brookline Historical Commission.

Arthur Gilman Archt.
Boston July 1858

Front Elevation & Section
Scale 4 ft to an Inch.

30b

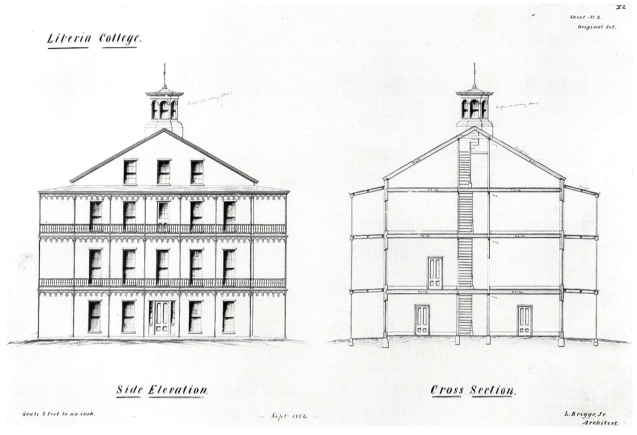

Liberia College.

Sheet N.º 2.
Original Set.

Side Elevation.

Cross Section.

Scale 8 feet to an inch.

— Sept. 1856 —

L. Briggs, Jr.
Architect.

31a

Luther Briggs, Jr. (1822–1905)

Born in Pembroke, Massachusetts, Briggs apprenticed to his uncle-in-law, Alexander Parris (*see*), from 1839 to about 1842, and then worked briefly with G.J.F. Bryant (*see*). Thus his apprenticeship was largely with designers working primarily in the neo-classical, Boston granite style. By 1844 he was an architect, in partnership for one year with Joseph Howard. In the 1840s Briggs turned out picturesque suburban domestic de-

signs under the influence of Downing's pattern books.

L. Briggs and Company was formed in 1871 and dissolved in 1887; thereafter the architect worked as a consultant until his death. Among Briggs's more imaginative schemes was an 1878 proposal to save the Old South Meeting House—situated on commercially developing Washington Street—by hoisting it atop a new block of stores and offices.

Briggs's graphic remains are found in scattered public and private collections.

REFERENCE: Edward F. Zimmer, "Luther Briggs and the Picturesque Pattern Book," *Old-Time New England*, LXVII, January–June 1977, 36–56.

31. COLLEGE BUILDING, MONROVIA, LIBERIA, 1856–1861.

31a. "Side Elevation" and "Cross Section" of "Liberia College," "Sept 1856." "Sheet No. 2 / Original Set." Signed: "L. Briggs, Jr. / Architect." Ink and watercolor on heavy paper, 12¾ × 19⅜". Society for the Preservation of New England Antiquities;

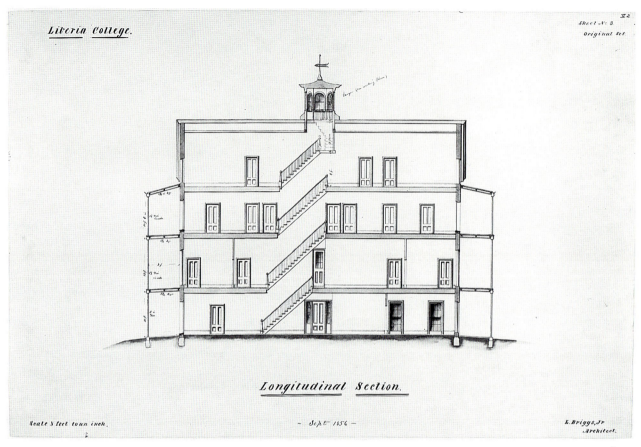

Liberia College.

Sheet No. 3.
Original Set.

Longitudinal Section.

Scale 8 feet to an inch.   *– Sept 1856 –*   *L. Briggs, Jr*
Architect.

31b

gift of Elizabeth Huebener, 1937.

31b. "Longitudinal Section" of "Liberia College," "Sept 1856." "Sheet No. 3 / Original Set." Signed: "L. Briggs, Jr. / Architect." Ink and watercolor on heavy paper, 12¾ × 19⅜". Society for the Preservation of New England Antiquities; gift of Elizabeth Huebener, 1937.

31c. "1st Story" plan of "Liberia College," "Sept 1856." "Sheet No. 4 / Original Set." Signed: "L. Briggs, Jr. / Architect." Ink and watercolor on heavy paper, 12¾ × 19⅜". Society for the Preservation of New England An-

tiquities; gift of Elizabeth Huebener, 1937.

31d. "Working Plans[, elevation, and framing details] of Observatory" for "Liberia College," "Oct. 1856." "Sheet No. 12 / Original Set." Signed: "L. Briggs, Jr, Architect." Ink and watercolor on heavy paper, 12¾ × 19⅜". Society for the Preservation of New England Antiquities; gift of Elizabeth Huebener, 1937.

The controversial American Colonization Society was founded in 1816, and the first colonists (freed American

slaves) were sent to West Africa in 1820. In 1822 Monrovia was established on Cape Mesurado in what became independent Liberia in 1847. The Massachusetts Colonization Society appeared in 1841, and in 1849 its managers resolved to support the creation of an institution of higher learning in the country with funds raised in the United States. The Trustees of Donations for Education in Liberia was incorporated in 1850. Its first president (1850–1855; trustee to 1859) was the architect's kinsman, George Nixon Briggs, Governor of Massa-

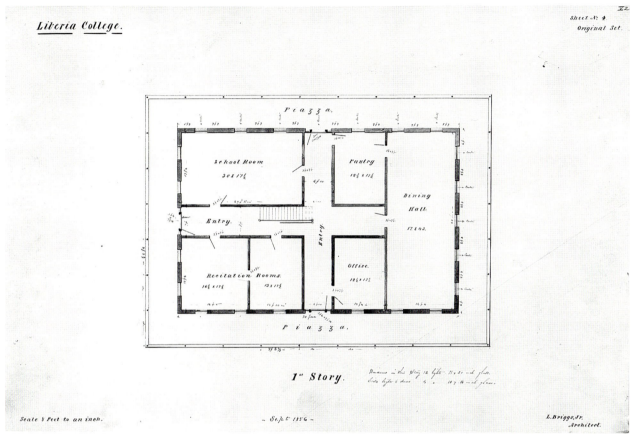

Liberia College.

Piazza.

School Room
30 x 17½

Pantry
12⅔ x 17½

Dining Hall
17 x 43

Entry.

Entry

Recitation Rooms.
16⅔ x 17½   13 x 17½

Office.
12⅔ x 17½

Piazza.

1" Story.

Scale 8 Feet to an inch.   ~ Sept 1856 ~   L. Briggs, Jr.
Architect.

chusetts. The Liberian legislature established the college in 1851; by 1855 $22,000 had been raised. According to Allen's history, in the next year "plans were drawn for a brick, three-story building, seventy feet long by forty-five feet wide. . . . A ship was chartered, ballasted with brick and loaded with other building material. She sailed December 28, 1856." After some delays, the cornerstone was laid in Monrovia on 25 January 1858, and after considerably more delay, the structure was roofed by April 1861.

Although the frontispiece to the publication of the inaugural ceremonies of 1862, an elevation engraved on wood in Boston, shows a building much like that which appears in these drawings and was presumably made from them, according to the photographs in Allen's history the finished product had all the glaring earmarks of the unsupervised construction it certainly was. The gabled, three-storied brick box surrounded by galleries and marked by an "observatory" envisioned by these drawings was built, but with the number of dormers multiplied, the observatory awkwardly altered, and the gallery supports dangerously thin.

These are four sheets of a set of twelve originals (No. 1 is missing). They are, therefore, the masters retained by the office while copies presumably went out on the chartered ship. They are basic, ruled-line orthographics representing a simple, substantial building.

REFERENCES: *Proceedings at the Inauguration of Liberia College at Monrovia, January 23, 1862*; Gardner W. Allen, *The Trustees of Donations for Education in Liberia*, Boston, 1923.

Liberia College.

Working Plan of Observatory.

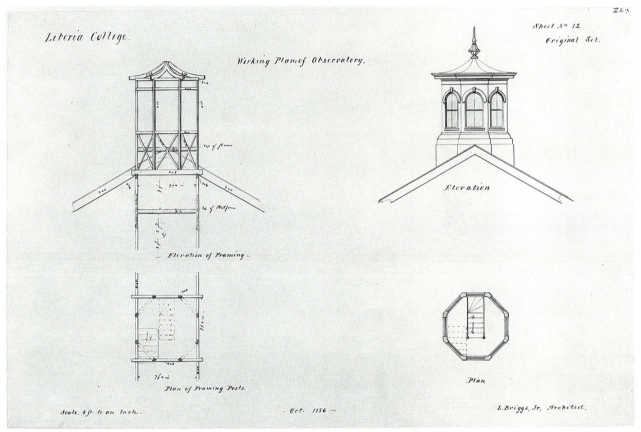

Elevation of Framing.

Elevation

Plan of Framing Posts.

Plan

Scale, 4 ft. to an Inch. — Oct. 1856 — L. Briggs, Jr, Architect.

31d

32. THAYER PUBLIC LIBRARY,
BRAINTREE, MASSACHUSETTS,
1871 (unbuilt competition [?] project).

"Front Elevation:" "Design for a /
Public Library / at / Braintree /
Mass.," "1871" (in tondo on tower).
"L. Briggs & Co. Architects / 35 Joy's
Building, Boston" (initialed l.l. and
l.r.: "S.D.K. Del"). "Style, Venetian
Gothic." Graphite, ink, and water-
color on heavy paper, 18¾ × 11″
(sight). Milton and Homai Schmidt.

Although there is no documentation
of a competition for the design of the
Thayer Library at Braintree, this
drawing suggests one, as the existing
building (now used by the municipal
waterworks) was commissioned of H.
and J.E. Billings (see) in 1871, contracted for in March of 1873, and
dedicated in June of 1874. Hammatt's
preliminary sketch, in the collection
of the Stowe-Day Foundation, Hartford, like Briggs's design, shows a
symmetrical facade with central
tower; his final design eliminates the
tower and takes on a decidedly neo-
classical format. Both architects seem
to drag the classical compositional
rules of their youth into the picturesque work of their maturity. Briggs's
is a presentation drawing enlivened by
pale (faded?), even, gray and pink
washes of a design combining an im-
placably axial *parti* and classical quoins
with the pointed arches, alternating
voussoirs, and iron roof crestings of
the picturesque. There is, at the Society for the Preservation of New England Antiquities, an unidentified
black-ink perspective of this design,
also dated 1871 on the tower. It shows
the building as a stark object floating
without setting on the white paper.

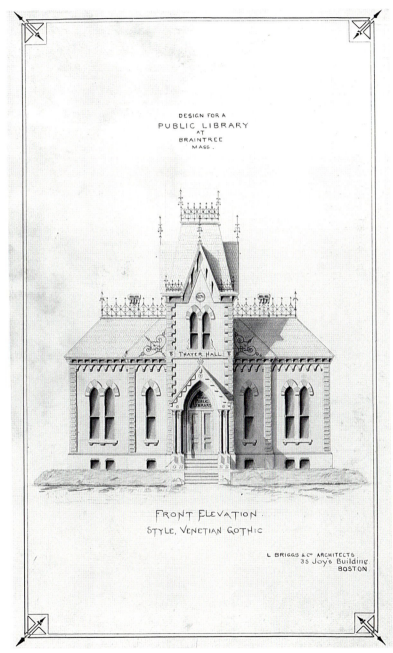

DESIGN FOR A
PUBLIC LIBRARY
AT
BRAINTREE
MASS.

FRONT ELEVATION.
STYLE, VENETIAN GOTHIC

L BRIGGS & Cº ARCHITECTS
35 Joy's Building
BOSTON

32 (see also plate 6)

REFERENCE: James F. O'Gorman, "H. and J.E. Billings: From Classicism to the Picturesque," *JSAH*, XLII, March 1983, 69–70.

H. and J.E. Billings (1845–1851, 1865–1874)

(Charles Howland) Hammatt Billings (1818–1874) was born in or near Boston, attended, but did not graduate from, the English High School, apprenticed in the 1830s in illustration with Abel Bowen and in architecture with Asher Benjamin (*see*), then assisted Ammi B. Young (*see*) during the construction of the customs house (Cat. 11). By the early 1840s he was ready to practice on his own or in partnership with his brother. Joseph Edward Billings (ca. 1821–1880) may have trained with or worked for Young but little else is known of his youth. He is first listed as an architect in 1846, when he had joined Hammatt in the Italianate design of the Boston Museum on Tremont Street, 1845/1846. It was a coming together, as was to be so often the case in the profession, of a gifted artist and an able engineer. In the 1850s they parted company for a number of years, with Joseph joining Charles F. Sleeper from 1851 to 1853 and then assuming for a dozen years the post of civil engineer at the Charlestown (later Boston) Navy Yard.

Hammatt's lack of training in the building trades probably led to his financial difficulties when he contracted to erect his design for the Church of Our Saviour in Bedford Street, 1846–1847. Unlike many of his predecessors in the profession in Boston, he was an artist, not primarily a builder: a jack of all designs as busy with book illustration (*Uncle Tom's Cabin*, 1852; *Little Women*, 1869) as with architecture. From 1851 until 1865 he practiced on his own and as a designer for others, such as G.J.F. Bryant (*see*) and S.S. Woodcock and G.F. Meacham, until after the Civil War, when his brother rejoined him. Their major work from these last years was the creation of the picturesque landscape and architecture of Wellesley College. Hammatt died before College Hall opened; Joseph went on alone until his death six years later.

Important collections of Hammatt's architectural drawings, for the most part small orthographic sketches in pencil or ink on tracing paper, are owned by the Print Department of the Boston Public Library and the Stowe-Day Foundation in Hartford. Scattered drawings are in various public and private collections.

REFERENCE: James F. O'Gorman, "H. and J.E. Billings of Boston: From Classicism to the Picturesque," *JSAH*, XLII, March 1983, 54–73.

33. COLLEGE HALL, WELLESLEY COLLEGE, 1869–1875 (destroyed by fire, 1914).

33a. "Sketch Plan of Principal Story of / Wellesley Female Sem[inar]y," north elevation, and sketches of roof details, undated. Unsigned. Red and blue inks and watercolor with graphite notes on blue-lined graph paper, 15¾ × 21″. Wellesley College Archives.

33b. "Elevation of North Front of Wellesley College," dated "Oct. 21st, 1871." Signed: "Hammatt Billings / J.E. Billings, Architects,/ Boston, Mass." Graphite, blue ink, and blue and ochre washes on heavy paper, 8⅛ × 27¼″. Wellesley College Archives.

33c. "Sketch of South Front of Wellesley Female Seminary," undated. Unsigned. Graphite, ink, and watercolor on heavy paper mounted on thin backing (onto which the upper part of the tower extends), 7¼ × 26⅞″ on 12⅞ × 20⅞″. Wellesley College Archives.

The design of Wellesley College was the crowning achievement of the brothers' careers. From a letter of the founder, Henry F. Durant, in the College Archives and a sketch by Hammatt for a gate lodge (an extant building now called East Lodge) in the Stowe-Day Foundation, 1869 emerges as the earliest date at which the design could have commenced. The Billingses provided Durant with the campus layout, the design of one and perhaps two gate lodges, and the main or "college" hall housing every activity of the school, including student and faculty living rooms, dining room and kitchen, gymnasium, chapel, science labs, social rooms, and so on. Cornerstones were laid in August and September 1871; the institution admitted its first students in September 1875. College Hall was sited on a picturesque rise overlooking Lake Waban. The architects' immediate model was James Renwick's main building at Vassar College, 1860–1861.

These are three of the several drawings, preliminary and presentation, which survive from the design process. They are considerably greater in size than Hammatt's other drawings in the Stowe-Day Foundation, but they are otherwise similar and for a building larger than any other he designed.

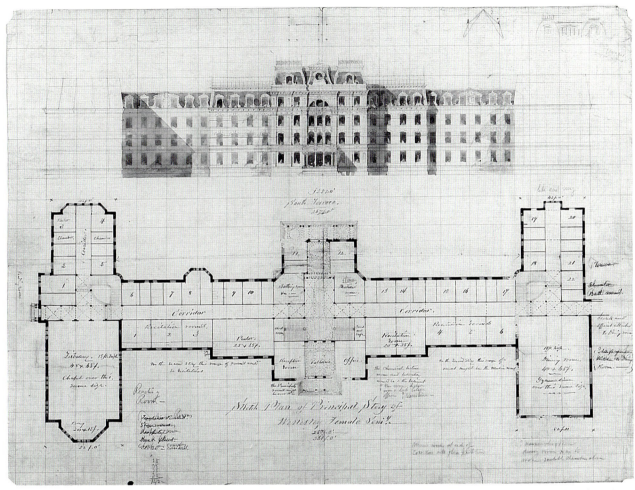

33a (see also plate 7)

The first sheet contains a plan and an elevation study for a symmetrical, Second Empire building, 361 feet long, with central and end pavilions at right angles to the long, double-loaded, spinal corridor. The projected mass was to rise three and one half stories, capped by a mansard roof. As we study this sheet we seem to enter immediately into the creative cooperation between architect and client. Pencil notations record problems and changes discussed at this point, presumably by the parties in consultation: where to locate the kitchen (eventually placed in a detached building to the west of the main structure), the placement of chemistry rooms in the basement ("?Sunshine"), and the single word "Tower" inked in at the extreme right (where the main tower eventually appeared). Further study was to evolve the polychromatic picturesque, stylistically Anglo-Franco hybrid that eventually stretched along the crest of the hill. This preliminary sketch is surely by Hammatt, the artist-illustrator and designer of the firm, whose stylistic and graphic roots penetrate to the neo-classical era in which he apprenticed (Cat. 11). Except for the use of colored inks and colorful wash on the elevation, the

ELEVATION OF NORTH FRONT OF WELLESLEY COLLEGE·

33b

33c

graphic here is a conservative, distant descendant of the ichnography/orthography-on-graph-paper studies of the eighteenth century, now perhaps best known from the drawings of Thomas Jefferson. There are other sketches from Hammatt's later career on this same graph paper.

Drawn after the laying of the cornerstones, the second, pencil study approaches the final design of the north front of the building, and

should be compared with the third drawing, the surviving south front rendered in watercolor washes. The building is now more than 500 feet in length, rising three and a half stories with four-and-a-half-story pavilions. The kitchen is in a building to the right. The introduction of the main tower to the right, a fleche rising from the roof over the chapel, and intermediate, vertically stacked oriels surmounted with spires, all add

picturesqueness to a design still rooted in its Second Empire origins. One thinks of the artist Hammatt as draftsman because of the extraordinary delicacy of the pencil marks and the accomplished use of different weights of line to suggest advance and recession of masses in an orthographic projection.

The third drawing is a colored orthography of classical details in a picturesque composition. It shows gray roof, gray window voids, and salmon-colored walls. The kitchen wing is a gray shape to the left of the tower. The 45-degree shadows cast by the projecting wings are the work of a lazy draftsman: they lie flat on the paper rather than suggest three-dimensional forms.

REFERENCES: Montgomery Schuyler, "Architecture of American Colleges X—Vassar, Wellesley & Smith," *The Architectural Record*, XXXI, May 1912, 512–537; Lee Ann Clements, "A New Light on College Hall," *Wellesley Alumnae Magazine*, 62, Spring 1978, 4–7; O'Gorman, "Billings," 70–73; Helen Lefkowitz Horowitz, *Alma Mater: Design and Experience in the Women's Colleges*, New York, 1984, 46–55.

Israel Porter Williams and M.S.G. Wilde (1862)

Both these men appear in local directories in 1859, Williams as a storekeeper in the Public Store Department at the customs house, and Wilde as a mechanical engineer at 23 Joy's Building, an address inhabited by several architects. Wilde's listing continues into the mid-1870s, but Williams's seems to disappear after the Civil War.

34. IRON FORT, BOSTON HARBOR (?), 1862.

"Plan[, section, and bird's-eye perspective] of iron Fort," "Invented May 1st 1862." "By Israel Porter Williams. / Boston, Mass. . . . Drawn by M.S.G. Wilde, 22 Phoenix building, Boston, Mass." Red and black inks and watercolors on heavy paper (now backed by linen), 19¾ × 29". National Archives, Washington, D.C.

Produced a year after the firing on Fort Sumter, three months after the launching of the ironclad *Monitor,* and two months after its engagement with the *Virginia* at Hampton Roads, this project probably reflects the local fear of attack by the Confederate navy or its allies, and represents a curious aspect of "*Monitor* fever." It is not clear from the drawing on which of the many Boston harbor islands Williams might have intended to place his metalic fortress (immediately after Sumter Fort Warren had been placed on George's Island); nor is the germination or the fate of this project known at this writing.

Not all building projects are the work of architects; Wilde's colored graphics have a charm not frequent in the drawings of his architectural colleagues.

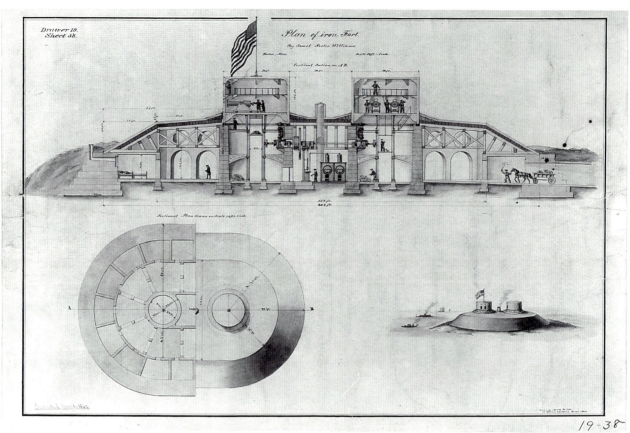

Henry P. Hall
(active 1866–1897)

No biographical information about Hall came to light during the preparation of this catalogue other than his listing in local directories.

35. G.T.W. BRAMAN HOUSE, BRIMMER STREET, BOSTON, 1867–1868.

35a. "Plan of 1st Story" of the "G.T.W. Braman Esq." house, "No 9 Brimmer St" (added in graphite), "Jany 18th 1867." Signed: "Henry P. Hall, Archt. / 41 Tremont St. Boston." Graphite, ink, and watercolor on heavy (Whatman) paper (watermark 1863), 18¾ × 12⅜". Society for the Preservation of New England Antiquities; gift of Walter K. Watkins, 1927.

35b. "Front Elevation" of the "G.T.W. Braman Esq." house, "96 Washington" (added in graphite), "Jany 17th 1867." Signed: "Henry P. Hall, Archt. / 41 Tremont St. Boston." Graphite, ink, and watercolor on heavy (Whatman) paper (watermark 1863), 18¾ × 12⅜". Society for the Preservation of New England Antiquities; gift of Walter K. Watkins, 1927.

Grenville T.W. Braman, treasurer of the Boston Water Power Company, moved from 69 Charles Street to 9 Brimmer Street between publication of the Boston directories for 1867 and 1868. His business address was 96 Washington Street.

Presented here are two of a set of five sheets for a townhouse the style of which represents a dramatic change from that shown in Charles Roath's design for townhouses of two decades earlier (Cat. 28). The graphic style, ruled ink lines with watercolor infill on Whatman paper, is usual in Boston at mid-century, and well known from the graphic remains of offices such as that of N.J. Bradlee (*see*).

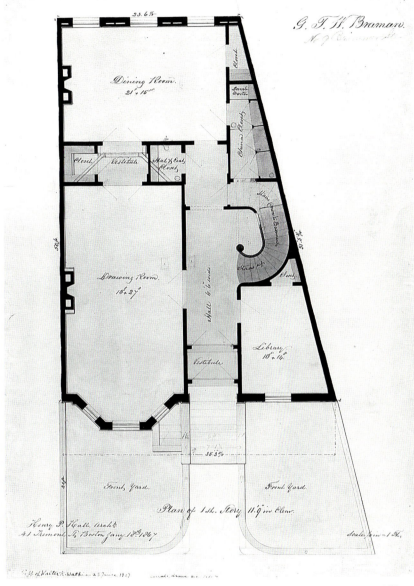

35a

G.T.W. Braman Esq

96 Washington St.

Front Elevation.

Henry P. Hall, Archt
41 Tremont St, Boston
Jany 17th 1867.

Scale ¼ in = 1ft.

Charles Edward Parker
(1820s–1890)

Parker was born in New Hampshire and first appears in Boston directories in 1847. He was associated with Richard Bond (*see*) from 1850 to 1853. He was the designer of many churches, including two in Newton, where he lived: the Auburndale Congregational Church, 1857, and the Church of the Messiah, 1881, as well as the Shawmut Congregational Church, Boston, 1864. In Chicopee, he also designed the City Hall, 1871.

REFERENCE: Obituary, *AABN*, XXX, 8 November 1890, 77.

36. THIRD CONGREGATIONAL CHURCH, SPRINGFIELD STREET, CHICOPEE, MASSACHUSETTS, 1868–1870.

36a. "Easterly Side Elevation of Chapel showing rear of Church," "Elevation of Church on Springfield Street showing part of Chapel," and "Elevation of Church and Chapel on High Street," undated. "No. 1." Entwined initials "CEP" lower left. "Return to C.E. Parker's Office / 8 Congress Square / Boston." Note: "Keep this Plan Dry." Ink on linen, 27½ × 20¼". Society for the Preservation of New England Antiquities.

36b. "Ground Plan of Church and Chapel," undated. "No. 3." Entwined initials "CEP" lower left. "Return to C.E. Parker's Office / 8 Congress Square / Boston." Ink and wash on tracing paper, 25 × 19¼". Society for the Preservation of New England Antiquities.

36c. Six sections and chancel ceiling details, undated. "No. 4." En-

36a

twined initials "CEP" lower left. "Drawn at C.E. Parker's Office . . . ," and "Return this to / C.E. Parker's Office / 8 Congress Square / Boston." Ink and wash with graphite notes on tracing paper, 25 × 19¼". Society for the Preservation of New England Antiquities.

36d. "Slating [pattern] for the main Roof of Chapel," undated. Unsigned. Graphite, ink, and watercolor on paper, 7⁷⁄₁₆ × 11½". Society for the Preservation of New England Antiquities.

The cornerstone of the Third Congregational Church in Chicopee was laid on 20 July 1868, and the church dedicated on 15 February 1870. The red brick and stone-trimmed pair of buildings (now the Federated [Congregational Methodist] Church) still stand above Market Square, corner of Springfield Street and what is now Pearl Street.

These are selected from a larger set of drawings (including those for the organ). Post–Civil War working drawings begin to look like modern graphics, with large sets of detailed diagrams in black ruled-ink lines on white linen or trace, once they are prepared with the intention of being photo-reproduced.

REFERENCE: Peter Webster, "History of the Federated Church," *The Chicopee Herald*, 9 May 1974, 15.

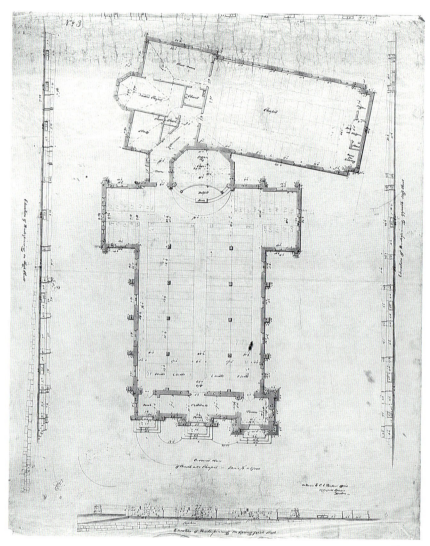

36b

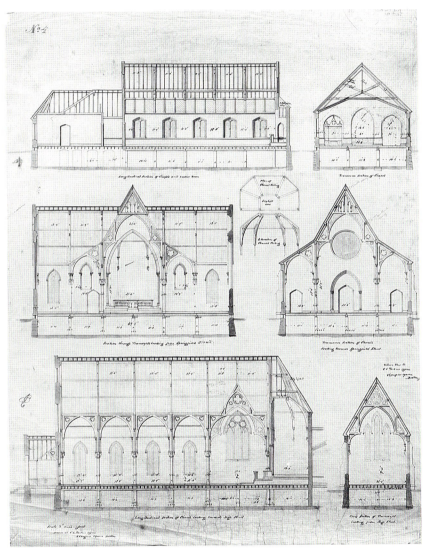

Longitudinal Section of Chapel and Ladies Room.

Transverse Section of Chapel.

Plan of Chancel Ceiling.

Skylight Area.

Elevation of Chancel Ceiling.

Section through Transept looking from Springfield Street.

Transverse Section of Chancel looking towards Springfield Street.

Longitudinal Section of Church looking towards High Street.

Cross Section of Transept looking from High Street.

Scale 8 lines 1 foot.

Put in decrease of Black Slates here

Put in only 7 courses of Black here

Chapel roof of Slating

This is the Slating for the main Roof of Chapel
1/4 inch = 1 foot.

36d

Plate 1 (see Cat. 1)

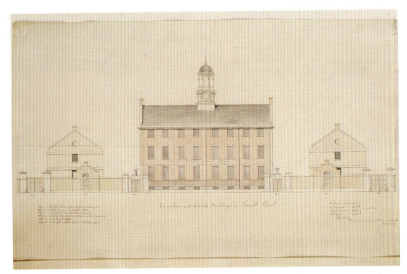

Plate 2 (see Cat. 7)

LATERAL SECTION showing CHALCEDRAL GALLERY.   LATERAL SECTION SHOWING ENTRANCE.

Plate 3 (see Cat. 15c)

Plate 4 (see Cat. 19)

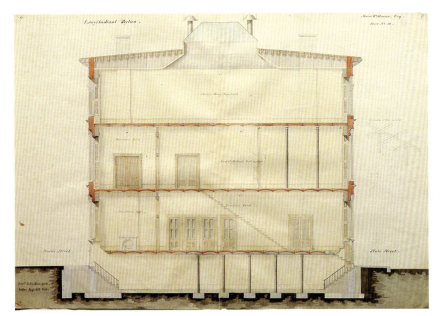

Plate 5 (see Cat. 22)

Plate 6 (see Cat. 32)

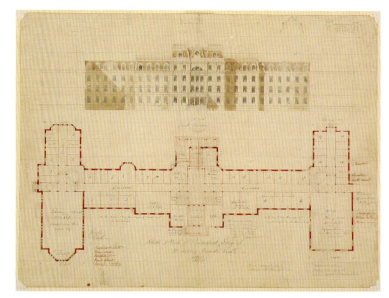

Plate 7 (see Cat. 33a)

Plate 8 (see Cat. 39)

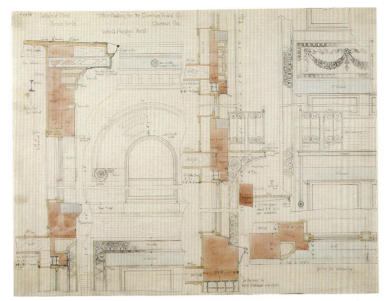

Plate 9 (see Cat. 47)

Plate 10 (see Cat. 48b)

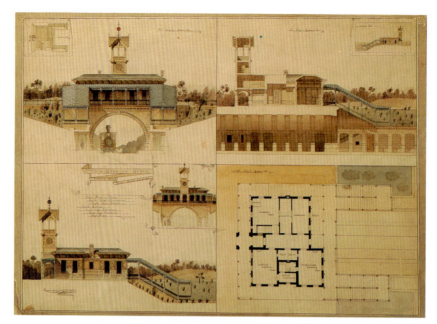

Plate 11 (see Cat. 55)

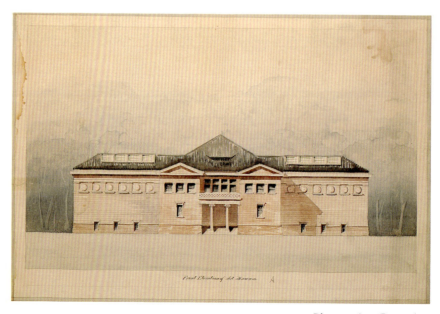

Plate 12 (see Cat. 59)

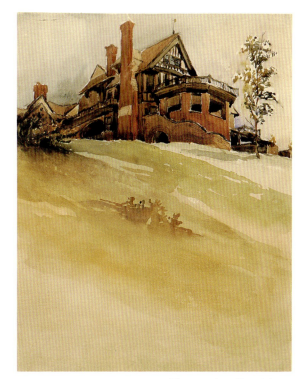

Plate 13 (see Cat. 65)

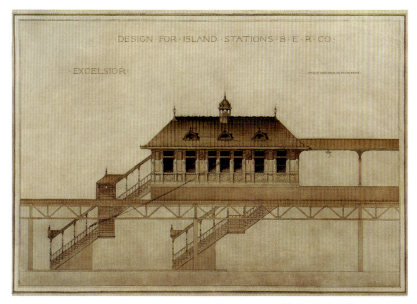

Plate 14 (see Cat. 70a)

Plate 15 *(see Cat. 72)*

Plate 16 *(see Cat. 77)*

Ware and Van Brunt (1863–1881)

William Robert Ware (1832–1915) graduated from Harvard College (Class of 1852) and the Lawrence Scientific School, then joined E.C. Cabot. In 1859 he entered the atelier of Richard Morris Hunt in New York, where he met Henry Van Brunt. In 1860 he began practice in Boston with Edward S. Philbrick, and in 1863 formed the partnership with Van Brunt. In 1868 he became the head of the first professional school of architecture in the United States, at M.I.T. (*see*), and in 1881 moved to New York to open a similar school at Columbia University.

Henry Van Brunt (1832–1903) was born in Boston and educated at Harvard (Class of 1854). He worked for George Snell for a couple of years, then moved on to Hunt's New York atelier. After brief stops at the Ecole des Beaux-Arts in Paris, the office there of Hector Martin Lefuel, and the Union Army, he entered the partnership with Ware. After Ware's departure for New York, Van Brunt continued to practice with Frank M. Howe, a talented draftsman, in an office located from the late 1880s in Kansas City, Missouri.

Ware and Van Brunt was a busy partnership, with Ware the engineering specialist and Van Brunt the designer, especially in the fields of institutional, ecclesiastical, and library design. The firm rose to prominence with its winning design for Memorial Hall at Harvard.

The Avery Library at Columbia University holds a series of sketchbooks by Van Brunt; other graphic remains are spread from New England and New York to the Middle West.

REFERENCES: Henry Van Brunt, *Architecture and Society. Selected Essays*, edited, with an introductory monograph, by William A. Coles, Cambridge MA, 1969; William John Hennessey, "The Architectural Works of Henry Van Brunt," Ph.D. diss., Columbia University, 1979; William A. Coles, "Van Brunt, Henry," "Ware, William Robert," and "Ware and Van Brunt," *MEA*, IV, 269–271, 373–376; John A. Chewning, "William Robert Ware and the Beginnings of Architectural Education in the United States," Ph.D. diss., M.I.T., 1986.

37. MEMORIAL HALL, HARVARD COLLEGE, CAMBRIDGE, MASSACHUSETTS, 1865–1878.

37a. "Half Plan of Roof Framing," "Half Plan of 2d Story Framing," and "Half Plan of 1st Story Framing," plus structural sections and details (some isometric) of the "Theatre of Memorial Hall / Cambridge Mass.," undated. Signed: "Ware & Van Brunt Archts." "This is one of the drawings referred to in our Contract dated April 12th 1875 Henry B. Rogers, Chairn of Bldg Comm Cressy & Noyes." Blue, red, and black inks, brown and red watercolors, and graphite notes, emendations, and sketches on heavy paper mounted on linen, 41 × 53⅜". Harvard University Planning Office.

37b. "Full Size Details of / Brackets & Balustrade / of First Gallery / Theatre of Mem. Hall / Cambridge," undated. Signed: "Ware & Van Brunt Archts / Boston." "NB Messrs Ware & Van Brunt would like to see one of these balusters before the rest are turned." Graphite, colored pencils, and watercolors, with graphite emendations, sketches, and notes on heavy brown paper, 86⅜ × 39⅜" (irregular). Harvard University Planning Office.

37c. Elevation, half plan, half section, and details of the "Brass Central Chandelier or Lustre in Sanders Theatre. / Memorial Hall of Harvard University," undated. Signed: "Ware & Van Brunt Archts." Black ink with red dimensional lines, and graphite sketches and emendations on stiff white paper, 17½ × 11¼". Harvard University Planning Office.

Ware and Van Brunt won the competition to design Harvard's Civil War memorial in 1865. Plans were ready in 1866, but they received important modifications in 1868 and 1871. Work began in 1870; Alumni Hall (the dining room) and the Memorial proper (the "transept") were completed by June of 1874; Sanders Theatre was finished by May of 1875; work on the tower ended in 1877; and the building was turned over to the school in 1878.

The Harvard Planning Office has a vast collection of drawings related to this commission; these merely sample what survives. The ongoing process of design is vividly revealed in these sheets, on which carefully drafted diagrams become starting points for further discussion, preserved in graphite tracks left by pencils in the hands of various draftsmen. Some of these are rapidly sketched perspective examinations, or three-dimensional "proofs," of two-dimensional elevations. The appeal in such drawings lies in their preservation of the evolution of formal characteristics which will finally

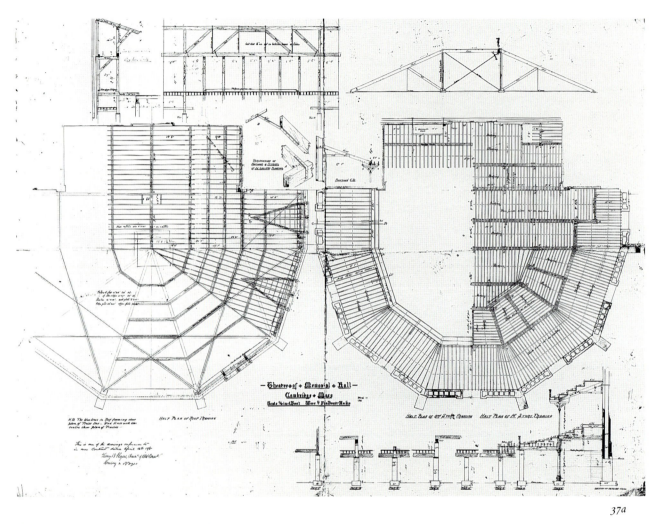

Theatre of Memorial Hall
Cambridge Mass
Scale ¼ in 1 foot   Ware & Van Brunt Archs

HALF PLAN OF ROOF FRAMING

HALF PLAN OF 2ND STORY FRAMING   HALF PLAN OF 1ST STORY FRAMING

37a

become the finished design. The third drawing suggests the totality of the design process as the architects create appointments down to the smallest (or in the case of this 24-foot high light fixture, largest) details. During the course of the century, architectural drawings gradually become more plentiful, more detailed, more impressive in size, and often possess more useful historical information than earlier graphics.

REFERENCE: Bainbridge Bunting (completed and edited by Margaret Henderson Floyd), *Harvard. An Architectural History*, Cambridge MA, 1985, 86–92.

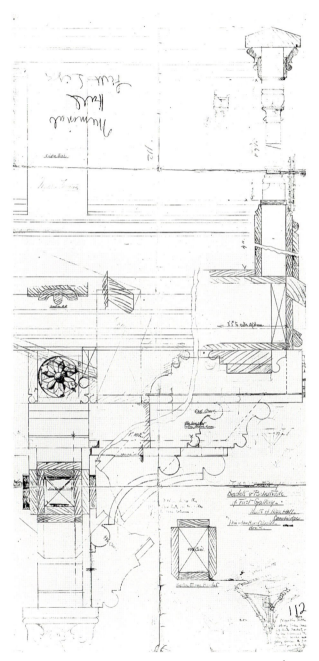

Memorial Hall. First Gall.

Full Size Detail of
Brackets & Balustrade
of First Gallery.

Mem'l & Hall
Cambridge

112

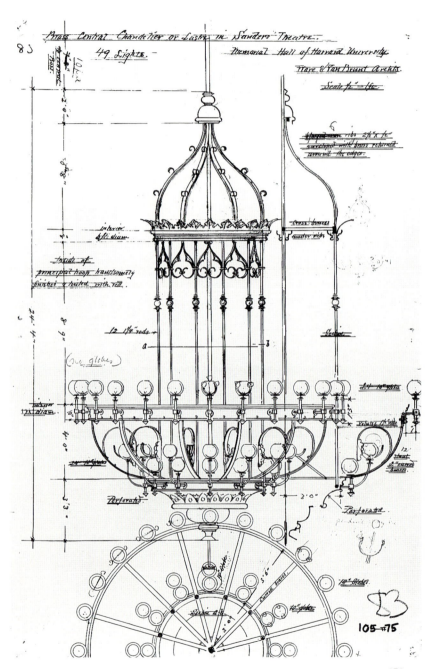

Brass Central Chandelier or Lustre in Sanders Theatre.

49 Lights.   Memorial Hall of Harvard University

Ware & Van Brunt Archts.

37c

Cummings and Sears (1867–1890)

The firm consisted of Charles Amos Cummings (1833–1905), born in Boston and educated at Rensselaer Polytechnical Institute (Class of 1853), and William Thomas Sears (1837–1920), born in New Bedford, Massachusetts. Each had some training in the office of G.J.F. Bryant (*see*). In 1890 Cummings left the profession to write about architecture and its history, while Sears went on practicing on his own until his death. Few drawings by this firm are known.

REFERENCE: Cynthia Zaitzevsky, "Cummings and Sears," *MEA*, I, 481–482.

38. NEW OLD SOUTH CHURCH, COPLEY SQUARE, BOSTON, 1874–1876 (unexecuted alternate design).

"Perspective View of Alternative Design, on the same plan," undated. Signed with entwined initials ("A.F." [?]), lower left. Watercolor on heavy (Whatman) paper (watermark 1865), 21⅛ × 24⅞". Society for the Preservation of New England Antiquities.

Although this drawing is unidentified by name, date, or architect, the site, what can be judged of its plan, the tower and roof pinnacle, and porch clearly point to a variant scheme for the church on Copley Square. New Old South was designed in 1874 and remains one of Boston's most prominent monuments of the High Victorian Gothic style, that polychromatic picturesque eclectic mode inspired by John Ruskin's love of Venetian building. It sits on its cruciform plan on the corner of Boylston and Dartmouth, with its tower rising above an asymmetrical entrance down Boylston and dividing church from parish house, its cupola rising above its intersecting roofs, and its porch of pointed arches with voussoirs of alternating color occupying the re-entrant angle at the street corner.

This is a typical watercolor presentation perspective of the post–Civil War era; typical, too, is its execution by a renderer who is not necessarily the designer or even a member of the credited firm. The renderer here is identified by unfamiliar initials; the projects Cummings and Sears published in Boston's *Architectural Sketch Book* and the *AABN* in the middle and late 1870s were drawn by Samuel J. Brown, an architect who also worked for other firms, both local and out of town (Cat. 49). As the *AABN* put it in 1880, "when an architect's drawings are signed by the draughtsman, it often means that he is not the fixed employee of the architect, but is established in an independent business."

REFERENCES: *The Architectural Sketch Book*, Boston: James R. Osgood, 4 vols., 1873–1876, *passim; AABN*, VII, 10 April 1880, 157.

PERSPECTIVE VIEW OF ALTERNATIVE DESIGN,

ON THE SAME PLAN.

Theodore O. Langerfeldt (?–1906)

Langerfeldt is listed in the Boston directories as an architect from 1870 to 1874 and as a watercolor artist for the next 30 years. He appears as the renderer of projects by several other architects in the Boston *Architectural Sketch Book* from 1873 to 1875 (signing his views with his initials) and may have worked largely as a professional architectural "renderer" or "perspectivist." His name appears on many drawings of this period.

REFERENCE: *The Architectural Sketch Book*, Boston: James R. Osgood, 4 vols., 1873–1876, *passim.*

39. UNIDENTIFIED CHURCH, undated (ca. 1870s).

Exterior perspective of an unidentified church, undated. Initialed "T.O.L." lower left. Graphite, ink, gouache, and watercolor on heavy paper, 15½ × 22″ (irregular). Earle G. Shettleworth, Jr.

Langerfeldt's is a splendid rendering of a generic High Victorian Gothic (or better—as it is American and not English—polychromatic picturesque) church with pronounced vertical proportions, pointed details, arches of alternating brick and stone voussoirs, asymmetrical tower, and iron roof crestings. The full richness of the prescriptive perspective common by the late 1860s is evident here. This is a fine example of the artistically rendered architectural drawing of the post–Civil War era. As the journals of the time generally used black-and-white line drawings for reproduction, this was probably intended for exhibition rather than publication.

39 (see also plate 8)

Samuel F.J. Thayer (1842–1893)

Thayer was born in Boston and apprenticed at sixteen to J.D. Towle. He served in the Corps of Engineers during the Civil War. A founding member (1867) and first Secretary of the Boston Society of Architects, he designed, among other works, public buildings for Brookline, Stoughton, and Methuen, Massachusetts. as well as Providence, and worked at Dartmouth College. His death was a suicide.

REFERENCE: William H. Jordy and Christopher P. Monkhouse, *Buildings on Paper: Rhode Island Architectural Drawings 1825–1945*, Providence, 1982, 235.

40. CITY HALL, PROVIDENCE, RHODE ISLAND, 1874–1878.

Interior perspective of the "Central Hall and Staircase" of the "City Hall: Providence," undated. Signed: "Sam'l J.F. Thayer / Archt." Ink over graphite on white paper, 70¼ × 14⅞" (sight). Division of Archives and History, City Hall, Providence, Rhode Island.

Thayer won the commission for the design of Providence City Hall in competition with 21 other entries. The building, which still stands, was erected between 1875 and 1878, without the tower shown on the exterior perspective illustrated in Jordy and Monkhouse. According to the architect, the style of his building "is a simple rendering of the renaissance, adopted because of its natural tending to symmetrical arrangements, and the fact that in the chief capitols of the world . . . [it] has been most widely

Central · Hall · and · Staircase: · :City · Hall: · :Providence·

40

adopted for civic and monumental edifices." As finished, without tower, Providence City Hall is a close variant on Boston's (Cat. 26); both display generic Second Empire silhouettes.

The stair hall, rising five floors from basement to skylight and surrounded by colonnaded corridors, occupies the center of the square plan. The columns are of polished granite; bases, capitals, balustrades, and so on, of iron; the stair treads, of marble. The upper stories have been altered.

Thayer must have been especially proud of this ruled pen-and-ink drawing—which is one of the set of competition graphics and has come to light since 1982—because he published a heliotype of it in the first volume of Boston's *AABN* (1876). It is indeed uncommon as an interior perspective. His black-and-white graphic continues a trend toward reproducible pen-and-ink drawings that marks the 1870s and 1880s.

REFERENCES: *AABN*, I, 25 March 1876, 99 and illustrations; *AABN*, III, 30 March 1878, 110 and illustration; Eileen Michels, "Late Nineteenth-Century Published American Perspective Drawing," *JSAH*, XXI, December 1972, 291–308; Jordy and Monkhouse, 173–175.

Alexander R. Esty
(1826–1881)

Esty was born in Framingham, Massachusetts, and lived there throughout his life. He trained in the office of Richard Bond (*see*), then worked for G.J.F. Bryant (*see*). The bulk of his production was Gothic churches.

41. LIBRARY OF CONGRESS, ca. 1875 (unexecuted competition entry).

Perspective of "Proposed Congressional Library, Washington, D.C.," undated. Signed: "Alex R. Esty— Archt." and "Manly N. Cutter." Ink on paper, 21⅜ × 32¾". Prints and Photographs Division, Library of Congress.

The call for competitive designs for a fireproof library to be built on Capitol Hill went out in August 1873. Although 28 entries were received, the competition was reopened in the next year, when Esty submitted this unsuccessful Victorian Gothic proposal. The existing building, the design of Smithmeyer and Pelz, was erected after many revisions between 1886 and 1897.

The Library of Congress houses two drawings from Esty's entry: an elevation and this pen-and-ink rendering by Manly Cutter (1851–1931), a young Bostonian who appears in *The Architectural Sketch Book* during the mid-1870s as both delineator (for Esty and others) and architect. He moved to New York to work for Leopold Eidlitz and others shortly after executing this drawing. The black-and-white medium was probably selected for its ease of reproduction.

REFERENCES: *The Architectural Sketch Book*, Boston: James R. Osgood, 4 vols., 1873–1876, *passim*; M. Cutter obit., *Pencil Points*, XII, May 1931, 379, 392; Bates Lowry, *Building a National Image: Architectural Drawings for the American Democracy, 1789–1912*, Washington, D.C., 1985, 66–67, pl. 63.

PROPOSED CONGRESSIONAL LIBRARY, WASHINGTON, D.C

William G. Preston
(1842–1910)

William Gibbons Preston was the son of Jonathan Preston (*see*). He spent the year 1859 to 1860 studying chemistry at the Lawrence Scientific School, Harvard, and the following year in the Atelier Douillard at the Ecole des Beaux-Arts in Paris. He began work with his father at the Boston Society of Natural History building in 1861 and returned to Boston in 1862. The B.S.N.H. was conceived as a unit with the neighboring building (1863; demolished) for M.I.T., then in the Back Bay. From those auspicious beginnings Preston went on to create such important local works as the Public Garden bridge (1866), the Hotel Vendome (1872), and Mechanics Hall (1888). His practice, devoted to a wide variety of building types, was centered in the greater Boston area, but he worked as far afield as Ohio and Georgia. He was a charter member of the Boston Society of Architects (1867) and its treasurer from 1871 to 1902. He remained active in the firm until his death.

The Boston Public Library holds 55 folio volumes of Preston's drawings, ranging in date from 1861 to 1907. With the preserved runs of drawings from the offices of G.M. Dexter (*see*) and N.J. Bradlee (*see*), plus the volumes of George F. Fuller drawings at the Avery Library at Columbia University, and the collection of H.H. Richardson (*see*) drawings at the Houghton Library, Harvard, these form an extraordinarily dense matrix of architectural graphics from the middle and late nineteenth century.

REFERENCES: Boston Public Library, "A Survey of Boston Architectural Drawings and Photographs," Boston, 1974; Jean Ames Follett-Thompson, "The Business of Architecture: William Gibbons Preston and Architectural Professionalism in Boston during the Second Half of the Nineteenth Century," Ph.D. diss., Boston University, 1986.

42. BOSTON SOCIETY OF NATURAL HISTORY (later Bonwit Teller; now Louis Men's Store), BERKELEY STREET, 1861–1863.

Sketch plan and rendered full-size elevation of an engaged Corinthian capital, undated. "Drawn by Garrett Barry." Soft graphite on brown paper, 20⅞ × 14⅛". The Gibbons Preston Fine Arts Department, The Boston Public Library.

The story of the design of the building for the Society of Natural History begins in 1859. After projects associated with Hammatt Billings (*see*) and B.F. Dwight were rejected, the Prestons arrived on the scene. First drawings were executed by Jonathan Preston (*see*). He was joined by his son while the latter was still in Paris, where he prepared an "original design" dated 1861. While later drawings bear an embossed stamp naming both men, the bulk of subsequent drawings are signed or initialed by the younger Preston. The building was dedicated in June 1864.

This soft pencil drawing, by an otherwise unknown draftsman, is not labeled, but comes from the volume containing other sheets for this building. It is a detail of the capitals of the main pilasters of the facades. The development toward optical drawing during the century is demonstrated by a comparison between this capital and that in Cat. 3.

REFERENCE: Follett, 47–57.

43. WILLIAM O. GROVER INTERIOR, BOSTON (?), 1871.

Elevation of a fireplace wall for "Mr. Grover," "Aug 4 1871." Stamped: "Wm. G. Preston / Architect / 15 Devonshire St. Boston." Graphite and blue wash heightened with white on gray paper, 14⅜ × 15⅞". The Gibbons Preston Fine Arts Department, The Boston Public Library.

Follett identifies the client as William O. Grover, who was a principal in the firm of Grover and Baker Sewing Machine Company. He lived at 17 Arlington Street from before 1865 to after 1875, so this may have been an interior decorating project.

A beautiful graphic in pencil on gray paper enlivened with white, this sheet exemplifies the fashionable richness of domestic middle-class interiors of the 1870s.

Drawn by
Garrett Barry

42

MᴿGᴿOVER

44. JAMES F. BENNETT HOUSE, CAMBRIDGE, MASSACHUSETTS, 1871–1872.

Full-scale profiles of "Cornices / of / Mr. Bennett's House, / Cambridge," "Feb 3 1872." Stamped: "Wm. G. Preston / Architect / 15 Devonshire St. Boston." Black ink and rose wash on off-white trace, 20½ × 15". The Gibbons Preston Fine Arts Department, The Boston Public Library.

Follett identifies the client as James F. Bennett, but knows nothing more about the commission.

Parlor and sitting room, entrance hall, and dining room cornices, presumably to be molded of plaster (the picture molding of the parlor is specified as "of wood"), are shown in bold contour punched up with wash.

45. CHATHAM COUNTY COURT HOUSE, SAVANNAH, GEORGIA, 1887–1889.

"Perspective Sketch," section, elevation, and full size details of the "Finial and Vane, Chatham County Court House / Savannah Ga," undated. Signed: "W.G. Preston Archt." Graphite, black ink, and watercolors on white Crane & Co. bond tracing paper, 20⅞ × 28". The Gibbons Preston Fine Arts Department, The Boston Public Library.

Preston, already at work on a local residence for George J. Baldwin (*see* Cat. 46), won a national competition for the Savannah Cotton Exchange in 1886 and became the leading architect in that city during the late 1880s and early 1890s. Through the intervention of Baldwin and other influential local clients, he was awarded in competition (held in 1887) the commission for

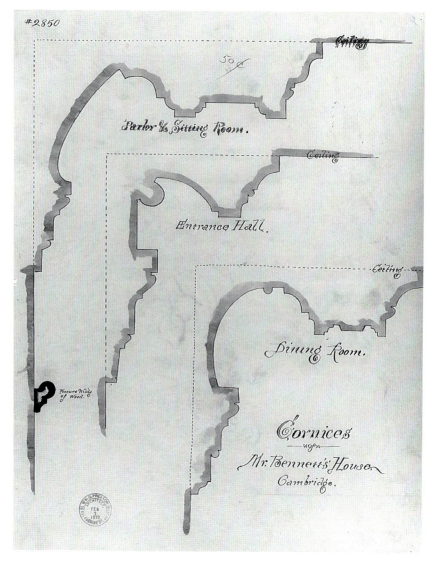

44

the Chatham County Court House. Construction began in June 1889.

This is one of a large set of drawings for this building. A preliminary sketch is dated May 1887; another, developed drawing shows a datestone with "1889." These depict a gawky, picturesque Romanesque pile in brick with terra-cotta trim. This sheet details the ironwork of the roof cresting. It is a characteristic product of Preston's office of this era: undated, with-

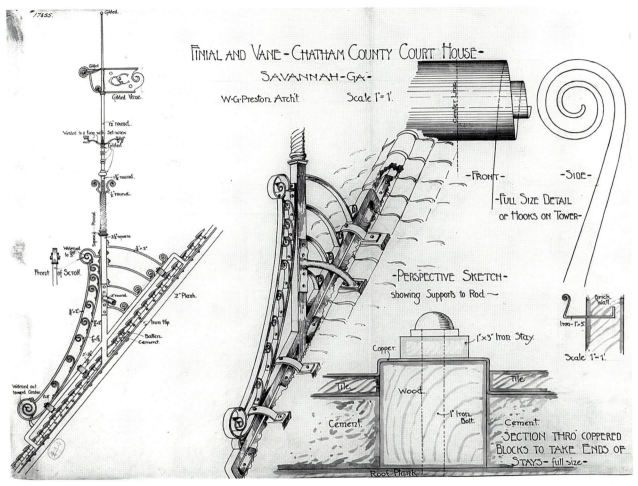

out draftsman's signature, in ink and color on white trace. It is an example of the graphically fully described details of construction and finish common to modern architectural practice.

REFERENCE: Follett, chapter VI.

#19.623.

G. J. Baldwin, Esq.

House at Alexandria Bay

46

46. GEORGE J. BALDWIN HOUSE, ALEXANDRIA BAY, NEW YORK, ca. 1890–91.

Presentation elevation of a "House at Alexandria Bay" for "Go. J. Baldwin Esq.," undated. Unsigned. Black ink on white tracing paper with graphite emendations and notes, 10¾ × 14″. (On verso: graphite sketches of a boat house.) The Gib-

bons Preston Fine Arts Department, The Boston Public Library.

Wealthy George J. Baldwin was a leading Savannah resident and the nephew and protégé of Boston's Loammi Baldwin. Preston also designed his Savannah house and did studies for a house (unbuilt?) in Asheville, North Carolina.

This is one of a set of fifteen draw-

ings by Preston for a rough stone and shingle, Queen Anne house at Alexandria Bay, New York, on the St. Lawrence River across and downstream from Kingston, Ontario. None is dated. The gifted draftsman (Preston?) has here produced a lively, scratchy free-hand pen-and-ink sketch that is characteristic of renderings of the shingled era. Despite the orthogonal projection and economical, black-

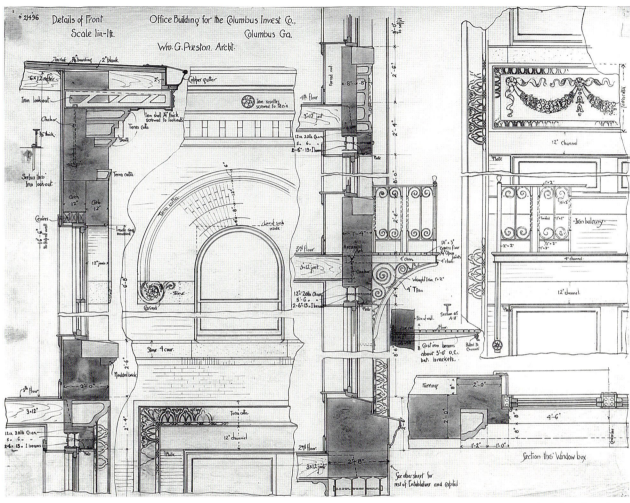

47 (see also plate 9)

and-white rendering, he manages to capture much of the feel of the aestival, seaside ambience (cf. Cat. 23).

47. CONCORD INVESTMENT COMPANY BUILDING, COLUMBUS, GEORGIA, 1890–1892 (unbuilt project).

"Details of Front" of an "Office Building for the Columbus [*sic*] In-

vest. Co., / Columbus GA.," undated. Signed: "Wm. G. Preston, Archt." Graphite, ink, and watercolors on white Crane & Co. bond tracing paper, 21⅞ × 28″. The Gibbons Preston Fine Arts Department, The Boston Public Library.

George Baldwin, a director, recommended Preston to the Concord Company in June 1890. The history

of the design is complicated due to financial problems which occasioned several schemes, and in June 1892 the project was abandoned altogether.

Other drawings in this set bear dates 1890 to 1892. They range from an early design featuring a cast-iron classical base, a brick, terra-cotta, and copper Queen Anne mid-section, and a brick Romanesque top story (the kind of eclectic pile that once gave late nineteenth-century architecture a bad name) to a more unified, Richardsonian Romanesque block.

This sheet comes from the later phases of the process. It exhaustively details the brick Romanesque arch, iron balcony, and terra-cotta panels of the front elevation in a richly colorful composition. Such a sheet of details produces a graphic that is architectural in a way that picture-making presentation perspectives never achieve. Its visual attraction is generated by purely tectonic values.

REFERENCE: Follett, pp. 205–207.

George A. Clough (1843–1910)

Born at Bluehill, Maine, Clough first apprenticed there with his father, a shipbuilder, then received architectural training in the Boston office of Snell and Gregerson from 1863. He established his own office in 1869, became the first City Architect in 1873, and returned to private practice in 1883. As City Architect he turned out a large number of public buildings, including many schools. His major surviving work is the Suffolk County Court House on Pemberton Square, 1895.

There is a large collection of Clough drawings at the Society for the Preservation of New England Antiquities.

REFERENCE: Edwin M. Bacon, ed., *Boston of To-Day*, Boston, 1892, 186.

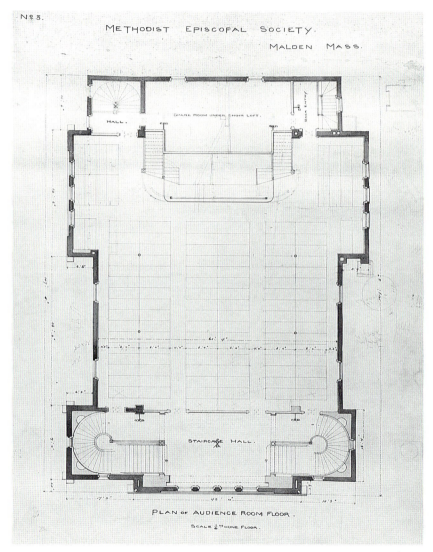

48a

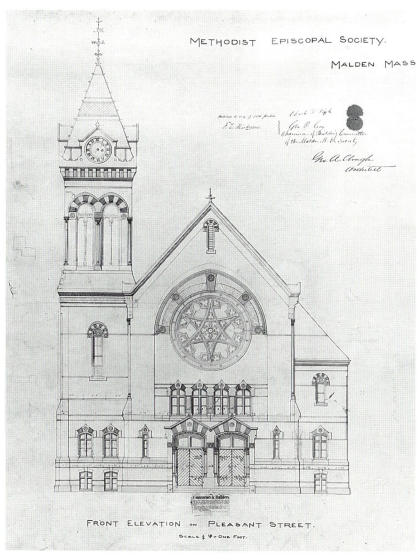

METHODIST EPISCOPAL SOCIETY.

MALDEN MASS

FRONT ELEVATION ON PLEASANT STREET.

SCALE ¼″ = ONE FOOT.

48b (see also plate 10)

48. CENTRE METHODIST CHURCH, PLEASANT STREET, MALDEN, MASSACHUSETTS, 1872–1874 (destroyed 1971).

48a. "Plan of Audience Room Floor" of a church for the "Methodist Episcopal Society. / Malden Mass.," undated. Unsigned. Black ink and watercolor, with graphite sketches and figures on heavy paper, 37½ × 19¼″. Society for the Preservation of New England Antiquities; gift 1987.

48b. "Front Elevation on Pleasant Street" of a church for the "Methodist Episcopal Society. / Malden Mass.," undated. Signed: "Geo. A. Clough / Architect." Also signed:

Witness to sig. of both parties	Charles W. Kyle [seals]
F. E. Nickerson	(Geo. P. Cox
	)
	(Chairman of Building Committee of the Malden M. E. Society

Printed notice to "Contractors & Bidders" and wax seals affixed. Black and red ink and colored washes, with graphite notes and sketches on heavy paper, 37½ × 19¼″. Society for the Preservation of New England Antiquities; gift 1987.

48c. "Transverse Section" of a church for the "Methodist Episcopal Society / Malden Mass.," undated. Unsigned. Ink and watercolor on heavy paper, 37½ × 19¼″. Society for the Preservation of New England Antiquities; gift 1987.

According to newspaper accounts in the Malden Public Library, the Trustees of the Malden Methodist Episco-

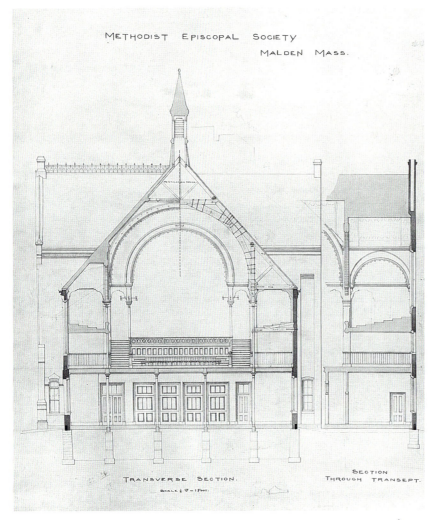

METHODIST EPISCOPAL SOCIETY

MALDEN MASS.

TRANSVERSE SECTION.

SCALE ⅛" = 1 Foot.

SECTION
THROUGH TRANSEPT.

48c

pal Society voted to erect a brick church with stone facings in August 1872, work commenced in December, the cornerstone was laid in May 1873, and the dedication of a church as shown on these drawings took place in May 1874. The building was razed in 1971 and immediately replaced with the present Centre United Methodist Church.

These are three of a set of nine sheets for an eclectic, or "round arched Gothic" church, to borrow a phrase from Henry-Russell Hitchcock. Clough uses traditional heavy paper rather than the new tracing cloth or linen. The size of the sheets and the masterful draftsmanship make for an impressive presentation. The signatures, seals, and bidders' notice affixed to the front elevation mark the function of these drawings as legal, contract documents.

49. MUNICIPAL WATER WORKS BUILDING, CHESTNUT HILL, MASSACHUSETTS, 1877.

Perspective, "1877." Signed: "Geo. A. Clough / City Archt." Also signed: "Samuel J. Brown, / Del." Watercolor on paper, 16½ × 18½" (sight). Society for the Preservation of New England Antiquities; gift of Earle G. Shettleworth, Jr., 1987.

The building was erected much as shown here, with the addition of ventilators on the roof. A stylistic combination of Romanesque arches and Néo-Grec details, the monochromatic design is enlivened by the contrast between rock-faced granite base and dressed limestone walls. It survives at the corner of Reservoir Street and

49

Chestnut Hill Road, opposite the Chestnut Hill Reservoir near Boston College.

S.J. Brown's pen-and-ink work for Cummings and Sears and others was frequently reproduced in the pages of Boston's *Architectural Sketch Book* and the *AABN* during the middle and late 1870s. Here he employs the loose watercolor rendering technique that became common in the 1870s when, it appears, a drawing was intended primarily for exhibition rather than publication.

REFERENCES: *The Architectural Sketch Book*, Boston: James R. Osgood, 4 vols., 1873–1876, *passim*; *AABN*, XI, 25 February 1882, 95; Eileen Michels, "Late Nineteenth-Century Published American Perspective Drawing," *JSAH*, XXXI, December 1972, 293–294.

H.H. Richardson
(1838–1886)

Henry Hobson Richardson was born in Louisiana, educated at Harvard College (Class of 1859) and the Ecole des Beaux-Arts in Paris, and began his career in New York in 1866. From 1867 to 1878 he was the nominal partner of Charles Dexter Gambrill. In 1874 he moved to Brookline, Massachusetts, where he lived and worked until his death. His major works, among the most important buildings in American architectural history, include Trinity Church, Boston, 1872–1877, buildings for the Ames family in Boston and North Easton, including the F.L. Ames Gate Lodge, 1880–1881, the Marshall Field Wholesale Store and the J.J. Glessner House, Chicago, both 1885–1887, and the Allegheny County Buildings, Pittsburgh, 1883–1888. Shepley, Rutan and Coolidge (see) succeeded to his practice.

All of Richardson's known drawings are housed in the Department of Printing and Graphic Arts, Houghton Library, Harvard University.

REFERENCES: M.G. Van Rensselaer, *Henry Hobson Richardson and His Works*, Boston, 1888; Henry-Russell Hitchcock, *The Architecture of Henry Hobson Richardson and His Times*, New York, 1936 (rev. ed. 1961); Charles Price, "Henry Hobson Richardson: Some Unpublished Drawings," *Perspecta*, 9/10, 1965, 200–210; James F. O'Gorman, *H.H. Richardson and His Office: Selected Drawings*, Cambridge MA, 1974; Ann J. Adams, "The Birth of a Style: Henry Hobson Richardson and the Competition Drawings for Trinity Church, Boston," *The Art Bulletin*, LXI, September 1980, 409–433; J.K. Ochsner, *H.H. Richardson: Complete Architectural Works*, Cambridge MA, 1982; James F. O'Gorman, *H.H. Richardson. Architectural Forms for an American Society*, Chicago, 1987.

50. TRINITY CHURCH, BOSTON, 1872–1877.

"Half Section," "Half Elevation," and details for "Trinity Church / Foundation of a Pier," undated. Unsigned. Graphite, ink, and watercolor on buff tracing paper, 18⅞ × 15⅝". Department of Printing and Graphic Arts, Houghton Library, Harvard University.

Richardson won the competition to design Trinity in June of 1872 and immediately revised his winning scheme to conform to an altered site. Completed plans were ready in April 1873, and construction actually began then, but biding by contractors demonstrated the need for more economy, and revised contract drawings were signed in April 1874. The tower, further revised in response to the objections of engineers, was finished by July 1876, and the church was dedicated in February of the next year.

Since construction began with the driving of wood pilings into the Back Bay muck, and this drawing is a detailed view of the pier foundations resting atop those timbers, it can be dated to 1873. It shows a crib of 12 × 12s holding the tops of the pilings and covered with concrete upon which are placed the pyramidal footings of stone-faced concrete. Although this drawing survives among those from Richardson's office, there is a chance this could have been drawn by a consulting engineer rather than an architect. Whoever did it produced a graphically clear presentation of a construction detail whose level of communication is increased by its visual appeal.

REFERENCES: O'Gorman, *Drawings*, 42–51; Ochsner, *Works*, 114–123; O'Gorman, *Architectural Forms*, 54–69.

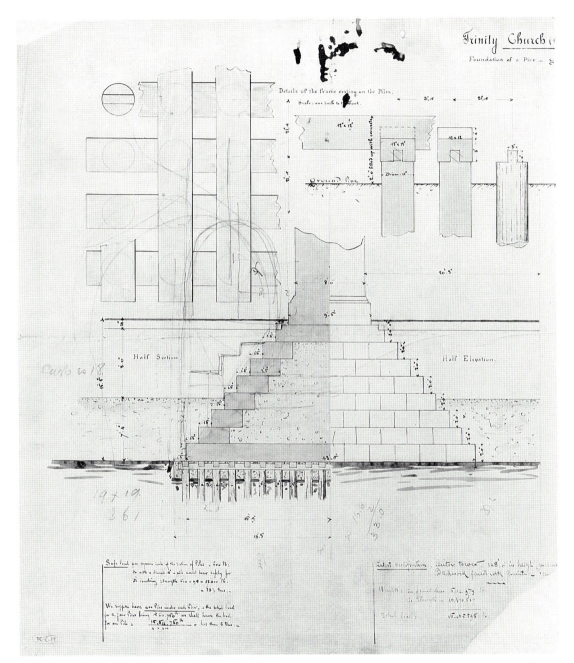

Trinity Church

Foundation of a Pier

Details of the Frame resting on the Piles.
Scale: one inch to the foot.

Ground Line

Half Section | Half Elevation.

51. OLD COLONY RAILROAD STATION, NORTH EASTON, MASSACHUSETTS, 1881–1884.

Preliminary plan and elevations, undated. Unsigned. Graphite on blue laid stationery paper, 5¾ × 5⅛″. Department of Printing and Graphic Arts, Houghton Library, Harvard University.

Richardson's North Easton client, F.L. Ames, commissioned this depot late in 1881, construction began in 1882, and the grounds were landscaped by F.L. Olmsted in 1884. Ames then presented the building to the Old Colony Line.

Richardson's personal contribution to the design of a building from his office began with, and was frequently graphically limited to, such "ideo-grams," in which he investigated the formal possibilities of a given pro-gram, usually in plan and/or elevation (almost never in perspective). This was a design method he had learned from the *esquisse* projects at the Ecole des Beaux-Arts. In this preliminary probe he organized in the plan at the top the simple spatial requirements around an axis running from carriage entrance through ticket booth to track side. The weight of his pencil line in the elevation below suggests his characteristic concern for a "quiet" silhouette: he emphasized the horizontal direction of the controlling ridge of the hip roof. But the third, side elevation must have demonstrated a busy-ness of form he did not like, for in subsequent studies he filled in the plan to create a simple rectangle, and capped that with a hip of four slopes and one continuous ridge. In such autograph sketches we come as close to the act of personal architectural creation as we can approach.

Once Richardson had established the geometric organization of the building program in a sketch such as this, he turned the design over to his office staff. They worked up scale drawings which he continued to criticize (*see* Cat. 53).

REFERENCES: O'Gorman, *Drawings*, 178–181; Ochsner, *Works*, 270–272; O'Gorman, *Architectural Forms*, 117–118.

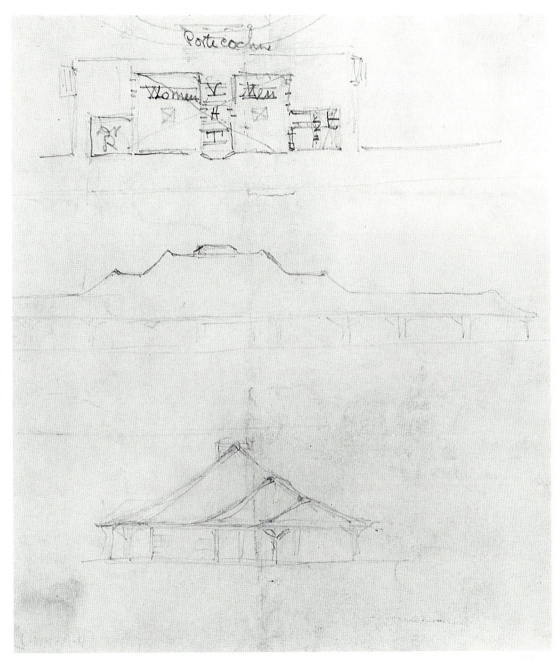

52. ALL SAINTS CATHEDRAL, ALBANY, NEW YORK, 1882–1883 (unbuilt competition entry).

"West Elevation," undated. Unsigned (red wax seal lower left impressed with initials "HHR"). Brown ink on heavy paper (formerly mounted on a stretcher), 41½ × 29¼". Department of Printing and Graphic Arts, Houghton Library, Harvard University.

In this full dress, monochromatic presentation drawing submitted in competition for the design of the Albany Cathedral in 1883, a competition Richardson lost probably because he ignored the condition that the church be Gothic, the architect's office produced an orthogonal projection of the front facade set into a perspective ambience. This was characteristic of Richardson and characteristic of the orthographic presentations he learned at the Ecole des Beaux-Arts (although it should be noted that the Albany cathedral presentation included a perspective as well). Uncharacteristic of the French school, at least in Richardson's mind, is the monochromatic presentation. In French drawings, he wrote in his sketchbook of 1869–1876, "form is sacrificed to color."

REFERENCES: "Design for All Saints Cathedral, Albany, New York," *AABN*, 14, 1 September 1883, 102; Montgomery Schuyler, "An American Cathedral," in his *American Architecture*, New York, 1891, 86–111; O'Gorman, *Drawings*, 52–59, 211; Ochnser, *Works*, 290–293.

52

52

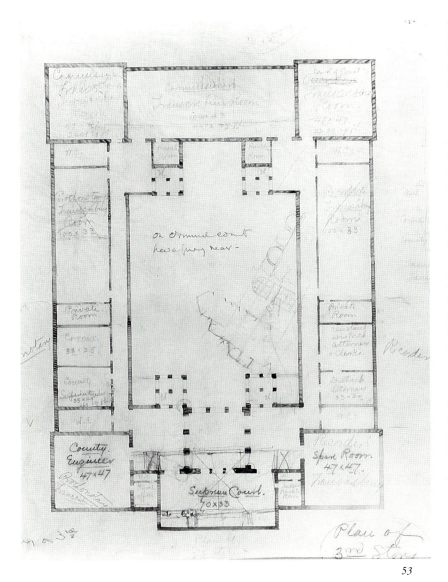

53

the result of a competition won by Richardson. Construction drawings were ready by that summer and the contract awarded in September. The courthouse was dedicated after Richardson's death, in 1888.

According to Van Rensselaer, Richardson's personal contribution to the process of creation in the office consisted of three steps: "initiative impulse, constant criticism, and final over-sight." The first stage is represented by Cat. 51. When the design was established in preliminary sketches, it was turned over to draftsmen who developed scale drawings such as this. Richardson then reviewed these development drawings, making comments and diagrams of the kind recorded on this plan. Here rooms are labeled in the architect's large, angular hand, and the sectional study presumably stems from the same source (or has perhaps been generated by a discussion between principal and assistant). This critical process eventually resulted in presentation (Cat. 52) and contract drawings (Cat. 50). "Final over-sight" signifies Richardson's close supervision of the rising structure; his lack of faith in drawings could lead to changes during construction.

REFERENCES: O'Gorman, *Drawings*, 18–27, 135–142; Ochsner, *Works*, 325–336.

53. ALLEGHENY COUNTY COURTHOUSE, PITTSBURGH, PENNSYLVANIA, 1883–1888.

"Plan of 3rd Story" and sectional sketch, undated. Unsigned. Graphite and terra-cotta wash on tracing paper, 21⅞ × 16⅞″. Department of Printing and Graphic Arts, Houghton Library, Harvard University.

The commission for the Allegheny County buildings in Pittsburgh entered the office in February 1884 as

54

54. MARSHALL FIELD WHOLE-
SALE STORE, CHICAGO, ILLI-
NOIS, 1885–1887 (demolished 1930).

Perspective sketch, undated. Unsigned. Graphite, black crayon, and
red wash heightened with white on
buff paper, 11⅜ × 19⅞". Department
of Printing and Graphic Arts, Houghton Library, Harvard University.

The commission for the wholesale
store entered Richardson's office in
April 1885. A brick building which
appears in early drawings eventually
gave way to the pink granite and red
sandstone block actually erected. The
contract for construction was awarded
in October 1885, and the building was

opened for business in June 1887, after
the architect's death.

The building's rosy color suggests
that this is a quick study for the earlier, brick version of the design (although the granite finally chosen was
also ruddy), which, if true, would
date it to the spring or early summer
of 1885. A brilliant drawing, it is
probably not the work of Richardson
himself, who rarely used color or
sketched in perspective, but of a
draftsman, perhaps Charles A. Coolidge. It has the look of an in-house
perspective proof of a design under
consideration, although it is close (not
identical) to the final form of the
building.

With rapid strokes of crayon and
brush, leaving much to the imagina-
tion of the viewer, the draftsman cap-
tured the essential characteristics of
the finished blockbuster building:
that it appeared to belong to another
age or another place; that it was liter-
ally outstanding, a landmark or pro-
montory amid, in Louis Sullivan's
memorable phrase, "a host of stage-
struck-wobbling mockeries"; that
it established a disciplined form
within a picturesque environment.
Here is graphically represented, with
economy and verve, the essence of
Richardson's contribution to late
nineteenth-century urban architecture:
the prismatically formed commercial

block wrought at an urban scale, a potent yet quiet "oasis," again to quote Sullivan, in an otherwise visually chaotic cityscape suggested by the graphite scribbles surrounding it.

REFERENCES: Louis H. Sullivan, *Kindergarten Chats (Revised 1918) and Other Writings*, New York, 1947, 28–31; O'Gorman, *Drawings*, 115–120; Deborah Nevins and Robert A.M. Stern, *The Architect's Eye: American Architectural Drawings from 1799–1978*, New York, 1979, 92–93; Ochsner, *Works*, 380–384; O'Gorman, *Architectural Forms*, 71–89.

School of Architecture, Massachusetts Institute of Technology, 1868 et seq.

William Robert Ware (*see* Ware and Van Brunt) founded the first School of Architecture in the United States at M.I.T. in 1868, with a program based upon precedents in London and Paris. With the arrival of Eugene Letang in 1871, the school's dependence upon the model of the Ecole des Beaux-Arts became entrenched. Letang brought with him a collection of Ecole student drawings. Gradually during the 1870s classicism was advanced at the expense of Gothic-inspired designs; by the 1890s the Beaux-Art's graphic style was the norm.

REFERENCES: *Technology Architectural Review*, I–III, 1888–1890; Caroline Shillaber, *Massachusetts Institute of Technology School of Architecture and Planning, 1861–1961: A Hundred Year Chronicle*, Cambridge MA, 1963; John A. Chewning, "William Robert Ware

and the Beginnings of Architectural Education in the United States, 1861–1881," Ph.D. diss., M.I.T., 1986.

55. A COUNTRY RAILWAY DEPOT, 1874.

Plans, elevations, and section showing a "Design for a Country Depot Employing Wood, Iron, Brick and Stone," undated. Signed on verso: "[William] B. Dowse." Black ink and watercolors on heavy (Whatman) paper (encapsulated), 24 × 18⅛". The M.I.T. Museum.

William Baldwin Dowse (1853–1917) of Boston received his B.S. in architecture in 1874 but apparently never practiced the profession. The *Register of Graduates* of M.I.T. gives his occupation as "Manufacturer"; he was associated, according to Chewning, with rubber companies in Boston and New York.

This is a two-level design. The stone is to be used as a base which incorporates a barrel-vaulted concourse at track level. The sheds, including those ramping between levels above the steps, are to be of iron. The building over the concourse, incorporating waiting rooms, ticket office, baggage, and so on, is to be of an exposed wooden frame infilled with brick and board. The latter is clearly inspired by Eastlake or recent work by Richard Morris Hunt.

Dowse quartered his sheet, and in three of the quadrants shows two drawings, a principal one at ⅛" scale, and a secondary one at either 1/16" or 1/32" which seems to be a visual commentary upon the main graphic. Two of the latter are rendered as if on small flaps pinned to the larger drawing, a

conceit with a long history in architectural presentation. The distribution of forms and colors across the plane produces a visually satisfying presentation. The French penchant for orthographics is already evident here.

REFERENCES: Shillaber, 13; Chewning, *passim*.

56. COLLEGE OF MUSIC, 1890.

"Thesis Drawing / [elevation and section of a] College of Music," "1890." Signed: "Elwood Allen Emery." Black ink and washes on heavy paper mounted on linen, 26 × 42½". The M.I.T. Museum.

Elwood Allen Emery (1865–1936) of Minneapolis held a B.L. from the University of Minnesota when he arrived at M.I.T. in 1887. The subject of his thesis was an appropriate one, for he seems to have been a vocalist of merit, singing first bass in the T Square Quartette and serving as president of the Glee Club (and secretary of the Architecture Club) during his last year. In fact, although he did practice sporadically (according to the M.I.T. *Register of Graduates*, as draftsman with D.H. Burnham and Company in 1906 to 1907, for example), he spent the bulk of his active life as teacher of vocal music at the Chicago Conservatory and privately.

Long before the date of this drawing, M.I.T. had come under the sway of the Ecole des Beaux-Arts. Handsome reproductions of characteristic, French-inspired student graphics can be found in the short-lived *Technology Architectural Review* of the late 1880s. Emery piles his classical composition toward the central axis, and renders it in orthogonal projection with, in sec-

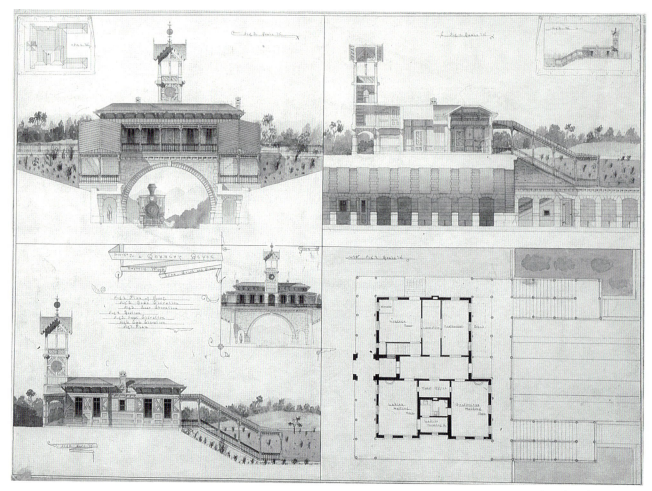

55 (see also plate 11)

tion, interiors shaded in a cool blue
wash to contrast with the warmer
tones of the sun-washed exterior
walls. Formal and graphic clarity are
thereby achieved, as prescribed by
current Parisian theory and practice.

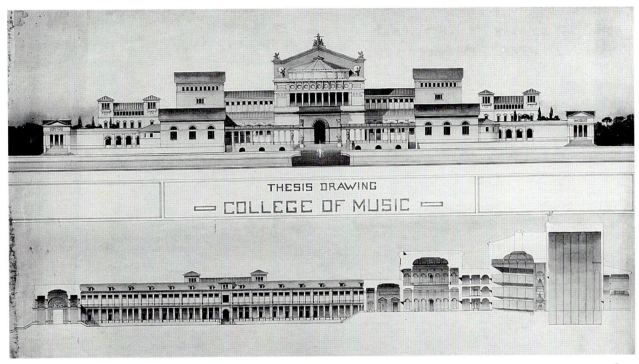

THESIS DRAWING
= COLLEGE OF MUSIC =

56

Hartwell and Richardson (1881–1919)

Henry Walker Hartwell (1833–1919), the son of the engraver Alonzo Hartwell, was born in Boston and trained in architecture in the office of Hammatt Billings (*see*) in the early 1850s. By 1856 he was in practice. The first of his partnerships, with Albert E. Swasey, Jr., lasted from the late 1860s to 1877, when Swasey went on his own and Hartwell briefly joined George Tilden (*see* Rotch and Tilden). The firm of Hartwell and Richardson came into being in 1881.

William Cummings Richardson (1854–1935) was born in Concord, New Hampshire, studied architecture at M.I.T. from 1873 to 1875, and then worked in the office of Ware and Van Brunt (*see*). According to the *AABN* for 1886, he was "well known as a clever draughtsman."

Hartwell, the engineer, and Richardson, the designer, achieved their greatest successes during their first two decades of partnership when they worked within the influential wake of H.H. Richardson (*see*). Residential design in the Queen Anne or shingle styles, small-town Richardsonian libraries, churches, and the occasional commercial commission comprised their output.

The few surviving Hartwell and Richardson drawings are scattered in various collections.

REFERENCES: *AABN*, XIX, 13 March 1886, 124; Susan Maycock Vogel, "Hartwell and Richardson: An Introduction," *JSAH*, XXXII, May 1973, 132–146.

57. UNIDENTIFIED SUBURBAN RESIDENCE, ca. 1885.

Side elevation, undated. Unsigned. Graphite and watercolor on tracing paper, 7¼ × 9¾". Society for the Preservation of New England Antiquities.

S.P.N.E.A. has two graphite and watercolor elevations and one pen-and-ink perspective sketch (initialed "WCR") of this unidentified, shingled Queen Anne house.

57

Picturesque domestic design from the 1880s usually appears in black-and-white ink drawings (or black-and-white reproductions in *AABN*), in which an accomplished penman can achieve the effect of texture and sparkle (Cat. 46). Here the tactility of the style is further emphasized by the richness of colorful, fluid washes. Even in an orthographic view Richardson's touch creates a vivid evocation of the projected house.

Arthur Rotch
(1850–1894)

Rotch was born into a wealthy and talented Boston family and early developed his gift for drawing with pencil and watercolor. He was educated at Harvard (Class of 1871) and in architecture at M.I.T., then worked for Ware and Van Brunt (*see*). From 1874 to 1880 he was in Europe, intermittently in the Atelier Vaudremer of the Ecole des Beaux-Arts in Paris or traveling (as far as North Africa) and sketching. On his return to Boston he joined G.T. Tilden (*see* Rotch and Tilden).

A number of Rotch's student drawings are held by the M.I.T. Museum; many of his travel sketches remain in private hands.

REFERENCE: Harry L. Katz, *A Continental Eye: The Art and Architecture of Arthur Rotch*, Boston, 1985.

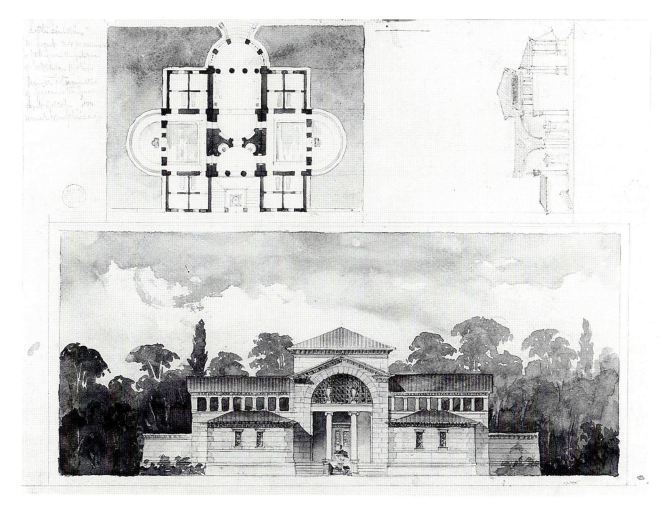

58

58. UN PAVILLON DE BAINS, 1875 or 1877 (student project).

Plan, section, and principal elevation of a "Bath House" (later hand; on verso: "Un pavillon de bains"), "[18]75" (later hand). Signed by a later hand: "Rotch Arthur." Inscriptions in English (recto) and French (verso; see below). Also on verso: beginning of a plan. Stamped "M.I.T. / Dept. of / Arch." Graphite and water-colors on heavy paper, 12⅜ × 16″. The M.I.T. Museum.

This drawing preserves Rotch's reaction to an assignment at the Ecole in Paris. The difficult-to-read inscription on the verso seems to preserve something of the program, or perhaps Rotch's thoughts on the character of the design. It begins: "Un pavillon de bains[:] Ce pavillon situé dans un parc à proximité d'une riche habitation de

plaisance serait tout à la fois un lieu d'utilité et d'agrément." It goes on to describe the number and arrangement of bathing compartments and a common salon.

Although this *projet rendu* is assigned by a later hand to 1875, Richard Chafee has dated it from an external source to 1877 and noted that it was rejected by the jury. An inscription in the upper left corner, not entirely legible, seems to record some of the jury's objections. It is written in English, however, not French, and may be Rotch's own summary of the criticism. It begins: "Little buildings in front not monumental & [take?] from importance of Entrance." Only one other comment is clear: "Out of scale." It was criticism Rotch apparently chose to ignore, for much the same arrangement of "little buildings" flanking the main entrance reappears in his design for the Farnsworth Art Museum at Wellesley College (Cat. 59) a decade later.

REFERENCE: Richard Chafee, "The Atelier Vaudremer and the Ecole des Beaux-Arts," in Katz, *Contintental Eye*, 35–41.

Rotch and Tilden (1880–1894)

Arthur Rotch (*see*) joined George Thomas Tilden (1845–1919) in partnership after his return from Europe. Born in Concord, New Hampshire, Tilden studied at the Lowell Institute, then entered the office of Ware and Van Brunt (*see*). In 1868–1869 he was at the Atelier Vaudremer in Paris. He joined J. Pickering Putnam in practice from 1873 to 1875, then teamed with H. W. Hartwell (*see* Hartwell and Richardson) until 1879. The Rotch and Tilden practice, which included suburban and town houses, churches, libraries, and other characteristic programs of the day, was cut short by Rotch's early death.

REFERENCE: Katz, *Continental Eye*.

59. FARNSWORTH ART MUSEUM, WELLESLEY COLLEGE, 1887–1889 (demolished 1958).

"Front Elevation of Art Museum," undated. Unsigned (Rotch and Tilden stamp on verso). Graphite and watercolor on heavy (Whatman) paper (watermark 1885), 20½ × 28⅝″. Wellesley College Archives.

Instruction in and the collecting of art are as old as Wellesley College itself. By the 1880s the School of Art was run by Ida Bothe, who headed the studio branch, and Elizabeth Denio, who taught art history. The success of their program brought with it the need for a building separate from College Hall (Cat. 33). In February 1885 a bequest from Isaac Danforth Farnsworth (1810–1886) made construction possible, and by June of 1887 Rotch and Tilden had been chosen architects over a number of other, unrecorded aspiring designers, with William Robert Ware (*see* Ware and Van Brunt) as consultant to the committee. The building was dedicated in September 1889 and pulled down in 1958 to make way for Paul Rudolph's Jewett Arts Center.

In his address at the dedication, reported in the *Boston Evening Transcript*, Arthur Rotch explained his design as reflective of the several uses it was required to serve. "The true character of the building," he said, "lies in the expression of its purpose and use, just as the exterior should reveal the arrangement of the plan. . . . The museum-like character is indicated by the high, unbroken wall surface of the exhibition galleries [toward the south], while behind them, above the low corridors, a frieze of windows announces a large [lecture] hall. . . . [At the rear] numerous windows indicate subdivisions within, of a less public nature. Here . . . the library, classrooms, and studios find compara-

tive seclusion." "The style . . . is Greek," he went on to explain. "Not a copy . . . but we have tried to keep in view the simplicity, the severity, the plain masses and concentration of delicate ornament characteristic of Greek architecture." Rotch chose his style on the principle of fitness, which he defined as "an architect's aesthetic conscience," and fitness here demanded a nod toward Greek building, "because of the traditions which so closely connect it with all European art schools and museums. . . . [T]he temple of art should sit upon a hill, so suggestive . . . in its beauty of the classic groves and mounts of the muses, [and] should be built from inspiration at the purest source of architecture. . . . This style is a logical and aesthetic necessity."

This is one of two preserved preliminary elevations in which the *parti* is established but some details and dimensions differ from the final building. In execution the project was simplified to produce a gray stone block of rather chaste and retarded Néo-Grec design, somber, chunky, and pinched. To some later observers it seemed a grim fortress of *Kultur*. In contrast to the even washes of renderings by earlier architects, Rotch's handling of watercolor seems to reflect the influence of the Impressionists in that he attempts to capture the dance of light upon solid forms. Despite such ocular use of his medium, however, Rotch follows French practice in using an orthogonal projection; he suggests nothing of the building's hillside setting. Except for the handling of watercolor, there is little to distinguish this from Bryant's Agassiz Museum elevation (Cat. 25).

REFERENCES: Various documents in

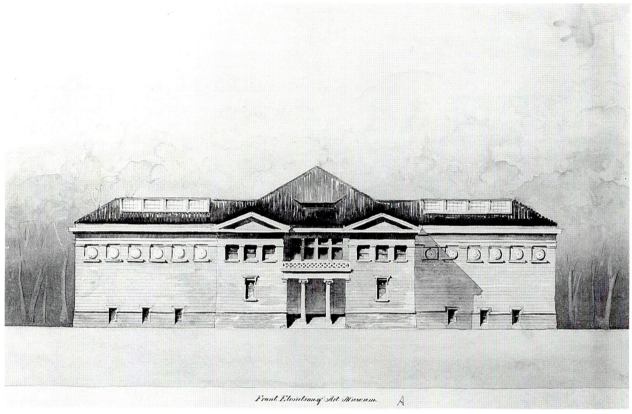

Frout Elevation of Art Museum.   A

59 *(see also plate 12)*

Wellesley College Archives, including clippings from the *Boston Evening Transcript*, 24 October 1889, and other sources; Jean Glasscock, ed., *Wellesley College 1875–1975*, Wellesley MA, 1975, 274, 326.

Shepley, Rutan and Coolidge
(1886–present)

The firm of Shepley, Rutan and Coolidge took over the practice of H.H. Richardson (*see*) at his death, and, under a series of changing corporate names, continues as a large, active office to this day.

Charles Allerton Coolidge (1858–1936) was Boston born and Harvard educated (Class of 1881). After two years at M.I.T. he joined Richardson. Charles Hercules Rutan (1851–1914) was born in Newark, New Jersey, and entered the office of Gambrill and Richardson as a teenager. George Foster Shepley (1860–1903) was born in St. Louis, educated at Washington University (Class of 1880) and M.I.T, then joined Richardson. The firm was created in the summer of 1886 to finish Richard-

son's ongoing works, including the Marshall Field Wholesale Store and the J.J. Glessner house in Chicago, and the Allegheny County Courthouse and Jail in Pittsburgh. With the commission to design Stanford University at Palo Alto, California, in 1890, the firm laid a sound foundation for the future.

The bulk of the drawings of this firm remains in its offices; there are some with the Richardson collection at the Houghton Library, Harvard University.

REFERENCES: Russell Sturgis, "She-

ley, Rutan & Coolidge," *Architectural Record*, 6, July–September 1896 (supplement); J.D. Forbes, "Shepley, Bulfinch, Richardson and Abbott: An Introduction," *JSAH*, XVII, Fall 1958, 19–31.

60. F. TUDOR HOUSE, BUZZARD'S BAY, MASSACHUSETTS, 1887.

Perspective sketch for "Tudor" house, undated. Signed with the monogram of Frank I. Cooper. Soft graphite on tracing paper, 3¾ × 9½". Boston Athenaeum.

There are in the Athenaeum collection two sketches by Frank Cooper of variant designs for a shingled suburban or rural residence for Tudor. Cooper (1867–1933) was born in Taunton, Massachusetts, and learned his profession in apprenticeship with Richardson and his successors in the 1880s. He practiced independently in Boston from 1892, and after 1914, as the Frank I. Cooper Corporation, specialized in schoolhouse architecture. Among the drawings from H.H. Richardson and his successors at the

Houghton Library, Harvard, is one for "Mr Tudors Barn"; an office receipt ledger dates the project to September 1887. These all presumably relate to the same project, with Cooper working on the design in the Shepley office.

The sketch shows a close variation on the theme of Richardson's Stoughton house in Cambridge, 1882, a house added to by Shepley, Rutan and Coolidge in 1900. It is an early indication of the influence of that seminal, shingle style design, and an example of Richardson's successor firm's recycling of his work (others being the triumphal arch which once stood at Stanford University, which was a version of early Richardson projects for Worcester, Massachusetts, and Buffalo, New York; and the Howard Library in New Orleans, a reworking of the unbuilt project for East Saginaw, Michigan). Ochsner published a similar pencil perspective in the Richardson collection at the Houghton Library as a sketch for the Stoughton house, but it is more likely a drawing for the Tudor project that is earlier than the Athenaeum sketch. Cooper

surely made this by laying tracing paper over that sketch and redrawing it with certain revisions (such as an arch let into the left gable and an entry in the tower). The soft pencil perspective is a characteristic and common in-house proof of a projected design.

REFERENCES: Obituary of Cooper in *Architectural Forum*, 59, November 1933, 34; James F. O'Gorman, *H.H. Richardson and His Office: Selected Drawings*, Cambridge MA, 1974, #41; Jeffrey Karl Ochsner, *H.H. Richardson: Complete Architectural Works*, Cambridge MA, 1982, #103b.

H.W.C. Browne (1860–1946)

Herbert Wheildon Cotton Browne was born in Boston and educated at the Boston Museum School, abroad, and in the office of Jaques and Rantoul. In 1890 he joined in partnership with Arthur Little (1852–1925), whose *Early New England Interiors* (1877) had been an early landmark

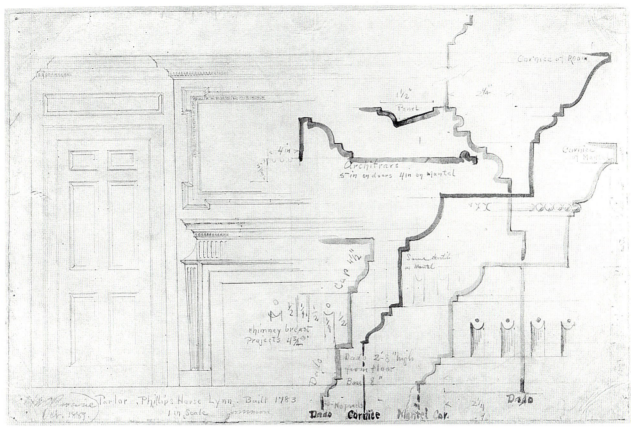

61

of the Colonial Revival. Little and Browne, an entity that survived Little's death, became a leading firm in the revived classical and colonial styles.

REFERENCE: Walter Knight Sturges, "Arthur Little and the Colonial Revival," *JSAH*, XXXII, May 1973, 147–163.

61. PHILLIPS HOUSE, LYNN, MASSACHUSETTS, 1889 (measured drawing).

Measured interior elevation and various molding profiles of the "Parlor, Phillip's House Lynn. Built 1783," "Oct. 1889." Signed: "H.W.C. Browne." Graphite and watercolor on paper, 11⅞ × 17½". Society for the Preservation of New England Antiquities.

Although interest in the colonial heritage of the United States quickened around the time of the Centennial Exhibition in Philadelphia in 1876, architects had already begun to record the vanishing monuments of that era in the previous decade. John Sturgis's measured drawings of the John Hancock house in Boston, 1863, and Henry Sims's of the Slate-Roof House in Philadelphia, probably 1867, record details of buildings soon to be destroyed. In the next decade these pioneers were followed by a host of students traveling and recording the architecture of the pre-Revolutionary era. Their incorporation of data gathered in new work resulted in the Colonial Revival.

This house seems to be something

of a mystery. According to the Lynn Historical Society, there was a Benjamin Phillips house before 1805 on Water Hill Street, but nothing else is known about Browne's subject at this writing. Profiles such as he recorded here were soon to be found gracing the interiors of middle-class homes in the greater Boston area.

REFERENCES: William B. Rhoads, *The Colonial Revival*, New York, 1977; Margaret Henderson Floyd, "Measured Drawings of the Hancock House," in A.L Cummings, ed., *Architecture in Colonial Massachusetts*, Boston, 1979, 87–111; J.F. O'Gorman et al., *Drawing Toward Building: Philadelphia Architectural Graphics, 1732–1986*, Philadelphia, 1986, 118.

Fehmer and Page (1889–1908)

Carl Fehmer (1838–ca. 1916) was born in Germany and immigrated to Boston in 1852 with his family. About 1854 he entered the office of George Snell as an apprentice and remained there some eight years. In 1862 he produced the presentation perspective of City Hall for Bryant and Gilman (Cat. 26). By 1865 he had joined T.E. Coburn in an architectural partnership; from 1867 to 1873 he was associated with William R. Emerson; from 1874 to 1888 he was on his own; and from 1889 to 1908 he practiced with Samuel F. Page.

REFERENCE: Samuel Atkins Eliot, ed., *Biographical History of Massachusetts*, Boston, 1916, VI, n.p.

62. AMERICAN BELL TELEPHONE COMPANY EXHIBITION BUILDING, CHICAGO WORLD'S COLUMBIAN EXPOSITION, 1893 (unexecuted project).

Perspective sketch of the "Bell Telephone Co. Exhibit / World's Fair, Chicago. 1893." On lintel of main portico: "The American Bell Telephone Company." Signed: "Fehmer & Page Archts," and "G.F. Bosworth / del." Ink on paper, 7¼ × 12⅝". Society for the Preservation of New England Antiquities; gift of Sibylla Young, 1983.

Bell was present at the Chicago Fair, offering long-distance calls to the East (the first Chicago-to-Boston connection occurred on 7 February 1893), but no list of exhibition buildings contains the firm's name.

George F. Bosworth practiced architecture in Boston until the 1940s. In this drawing he reverts to the largely unshaded outline graphics of the neo-classicist draftsmen of a century earlier.

S. Edwin Tobey (active 1880–1925)

Tobey set up practice in Boston in 1880. The Romanesque S.S. Pierce Building on Copley Square, 1887 (demolished), was among his most conspicuous local monuments.

REFERENCE: *Boston with its Points of Interest*, New York, 1895, 60.

63. YACHT CLUB, HULL, MASSACHUSETTS, 1894 (destroyed).

Presentation perspective, undated. Signed: "S. Edwin Tobey Archt / Boston." Gray wash on heavy paper, 18¾ × 30¾". Boston Athenaeum.

Although the architect provides neither, information accompanying the drawing gives Hull as the site and 1894 as the date. The building was indeed erected at Hull, that spit of land off Hingham, east of Boston. It stood at the foot of Hull Hill off Highland Avenue on a platform of fill projecting into Hingham Bay. Only the platform remains.

Tobey envisions his design for a four-square, hip-roofed and galleried, Richardsonian building with round corner turret and prominent dormers set at water's edge as it might look on a day breezy enough to delight the yacht club navy. The gray wash captures perfectly the dance of light and shadow across the volumes and surfaces of this shingle style building. The two figures and the boat at lower left form a chinoiserie vignette that seems to pay homage to the Oriental affinities of this American wooden style. This is a presentation drawing filled with vitality despite its lack of color.

REFERENCE: Hull Historical Commission.

G. F. Bowroth
del.

Fehmer & Page Archts
Bell Telephone Co. Exhibit
World's Fair, Chicago. 1893

62

63

Robert Swain Peabody
(1845–1917)

Peabody was born in New Bedford, Massachusetts, and, after graduation from Harvard College (Class of 1866), worked briefly for G.J.F. Bryant (*see*) and Ware and Van Brunt (*see*). The next several years were spent studying and traveling in England and on the Continent, including a period at the Ecole des Beaux-Arts in Paris. He returned to Boston in 1870 to form a partnership with John G. Stearns (*see* Peabody and Stearns), crossing the Atlantic on several subsequent occa-

sions. Peabody, the designing partner of the firm, rose to a position of leadership in the profession, serving one term as president of the American Institute of Architects, 1900 to 1901.

In 1873 and 1912 Peabody published groups of sketches made during his European sojourns. These and other of his graphic remains are in the collection of the Boston Architectural Center and the Boston Public Library.

REFERENCES: R.S. Peabody, *Note Book Sketches by Robert Swain Peabody, Arch't.*, Boston, 1873; R.S. Peabody, *An Architect's Sketch Book*, Boston and New York, 1912.

64. TRAVEL SKETCHES, 1868 and 1876.

64a. Exterior perspective of "St. Pere / Oct. 1868." Unsigned. Graphite on paper, 9 × 6¼". Boston Architectural Center.

64b. Detail of the exterior of a "Warehouse. / Lord St. / Liverpool. / By E. W. Pugin. Jan. 19. 1876." Unsigned. Graphite on heavy buff paper, 6⅝ × 3½". Boston Architectural Center.

Two of the many relatively small pencil sketches executed by Peabody during study tours as a student and afterward show him looking at old and relatively recent examples of English and Continental architecture. Such "student's notes," as he calls them in his 1873 publication, were characteristic products of travel by aspiring architects before the advent of the Kodak portable, roll film, box camera in the 1880s (and, eventually, the 35-mm camera). The forms and spirit in such notes subsequently found reuse in designs by Peabody as a practicing architect.

Peabody and Stearns (1870–1917)

The partnership was formed in 1870 by Robert Swain Peabody (*see*) and John Goddard Stearns (1843–1917) and lasted until their deaths a few days apart. Stearns was born in New York City but grew up in Brookline, Massachusetts. He was educated at the Lawrence Scientific School in Cambridge, and in the office of Ware and Van Brunt (*see*). Peabody, a gifted draftsman, was the firm's designer; Stearns, the engineering partner.

64a

Peabody and Stearns rose to the top of the architectural profession in the last decades of the nineteenth century, achieving its best work during the 1880s and early 1890s when J.A. Schweinfurth (*see*) was chief draftsman. The firm turned out more than a thousand commissions locally and nationally, establishing its primacy in the Colonial Revival but working in a wide range of other styles as well, and trained many of the leading designers of the next generation.

A large and largely unstudied collection of some 1,220 rolls of original drawings and copies of drawings from the firm is housed in the Print Department, Boston Public Library. There are scattered drawings in other collections.

REFERENCES: Russell Sturgis, *A Critique of the Work of Peabody and Stearns*, 1896 (reprint, New York, 1971); Boston Public Library, "A Survey of Boston Architectural Drawings and Photographs," Boston, 1974; Wheaton Holden, "The Peabody Touch: Peabody and Stearns of Boston, 1870–1917," *JSAH*, XXXII, May 1973, 114–131; Margaret Henderson Floyd and Wheaton Holden, "Peabody and Stearns," *MEA*, III, 380–381.

65. UNIDENTIFIED SUBURBAN RESIDENCE, undated.

Exterior perspective, undated. Unsigned. Graphite and watercolor on heavy paper, 11 × 8⅜". Boston Architectural Center.

Although unsigned, this is found among the Peabody sketches at the Boston Architectural Center, and is presumably by him. Although un-

WAREHOUSE·
·LORD·ST·
·LIVERPOOL·
·BY·E·W·PUGIN·   JAN·19·18/6·

CUT·STONE·DRESSINGS·
ROUGH·FILLING·

64b

65 (see also plate 13)

dated, this is clearly a house of the 1880s, as is suggested by the picturesque brick, wood, and stucco Queen Anne style, the exaggerated *da sotto in su* perspective, reflecting the influence of Japanese composition, and the handling of the watercolor, which may show some influence of the Impressionists. It was of a sketch such as this or of that in Cat. 66 that the *AABN* in 1886 wrote: "As with all Mr. Peabody's perspectives, the angle of view, the height above the horizon, and the distance and position of the vanishing-points, are chosen with care and judgment which we would commend to the attention . . . , and on the foundation so obtained he builds his effects of light and shade and color with confidence."

REFERENCE: *AABN*, XIX, 13 March 1886, 125.

66. UNIDENTIFIED SEASHORE RESIDENCE, undated.

Exterior perspective of a house "At Lobster Cove," undated. Unsigned. Graphite on paper, 9 × 6⅞". Boston Architectural Center.

This too is found among the Peabody sketches at the B.A.C. Water, rocks, vegetation, and picturesque silhouette of house amount to an evocative pencil image of a coastal, and presumably North Shore (Manchester, Massachusetts?), summer "cottage" of the shingled era.

67. HOUGHTON MEMORIAL CHAPEL, WELLESLEY COLLEGE, 1896 (unbuilt competition entry).

Exterior perspective of a "Chapel for Wellesley College," undated. La-

At Lobster Cove.

66

was Horace E. Scudder, invited competing designs on 9 June 1896 from Shaw and Hunnewell, A.W. Longfellow, Jr. (*see*), Peabody and Stearns, and Heins and Lafarge. The program outlined in Scudder's letter of invitation consisted of four parts: 1) cost, "including decoration, windows and provision for an organ, together with preparation of site," was not to exceed the Houghton gift, 2) "the building [was] to be academic in character, and especially adapted to worship, though not limited to one ecclesiastical order," 3) capacity to be 1,300 in chairs, and 4) "the acoustic properties [were] to regard women's voices." There was a choice of sites. Drawings, due 1 September, were to include "a perspective view from one or more points, a ground plan and such further details as will enable the committee" to understand the design. Each participant was to be paid $300 (their canceled checks still exist in College Archives). In October the contestants were notified that Heins and Lafarge had been chosen architects of the chapel; their Gothic building was dedicated in 1899.

Although Scudder's letter stated that all drawings were to become the property of the College, in fact they were returned to the architects. This presentation perspective was somehow overlooked, however, and now seems to be the only known graphic from the competition. It shows a domed, cruciform, neo-classical chapel with tetrastyle Corinthian portico and twin bell towers that seems to descend from Palladio. Although in style it differs from the winning design in an "ecclesiastical order," its plan was probably not very different from that which was built. The gifted

beled on original mat: "Peabody and Stearns Architects." Graphite and brown ink wash on cardboard, 23¼ × 31½" (oval opening in mat). Wellesley College Archives.

Just twelve years after the opening of Wellesley College, the chapel within

H. and J.E. Billings's College Hall (Cat. 33) could no longer contain the student body. In 1896 the heirs of William S. Houghton, a Trustee from 1880 to 1884, gave the College $100,000 to build a new chapel. The Building Committee, whose secretary

67

draftsman (Peabody?) limited himself to ruled graphite lines and a fluid brown wash to create a vividly evocative image. Judging by comments in *AABN* for 1886, brown wash graphics were common products of the Peabody office.

REFERENCES: Horace E. Scudder letterbook and related documents, Wellesley College Archives; *AABN*, XIX, 13 March 1886, 125; Jean Glasscock, ed., *Wellesley College 1875–1975*, Wellesley MA, 1975, 302–304; James F. O'Gorman, "Unbuilt Wellesley I: A Fragment from the Great Debate," *Wellesley Wragtime*, II, May 1979, 8–9.

68a

R. Clipston Sturgis (1860–1951)

Harvard-educated (Class of 1881) Clipston Sturgis joined the firm of Sturgis and Brigham just out of college. After travel in Europe, 1884 to 1886, he took over his uncle's practice in 1887, just before the latter's death, and went on to a distinguished career, including the national presidency of the American Institute of Architects,

1914 to 1915. He turned out nearly six hundred commissions before his retirement in 1920.

REFERENCE: Margaret Henderson Floyd, "John Hubbard Sturgis: American Architecture in the English Image," unpublished manuscript, 415 *et seq.*

68. TRAVEL SKETCHES, 1884–1886.

68a. Interior perspective of the "Vestibule between Cloisters & Chapter House / Westminster. May 24th '84." Initialed "[R.]C.S. [Del]t." Graphite on heavy paper, 14 × 9⅞". Boston Architectural Center.

68b. Measured drawing of the "Screen of Andrea Ocagna's Shrine / Or San Michele. Florence . . . Mar[ch] 25th [18]86." Unsigned. Graphite and watercolors on heavy paper, 14 × 9⅞". Boston Architectural Center.

Screen of Andrea Ocagna's Shrine
Or San Michele. Florence

Bronze reliable.

Scale 2' = 1' 0"

Mar 25th 86.

Full Size Flower.

shelf for Candelabra.

Floor of Shrine

outer Floor

68b

The B.A.C. has two bound volumes of 254 travel sketches by R. Clipston Sturgis, mostly pencil, ink, and watercolor, and largely from 1884 to 1886 (a few from 1901 and 1908). These include drawings made in Italy, France, Holland, Germany, and England (and a few of buildings by local leaders such as H.H. Richardson [*see*], W.R. Emerson, and Peabody and Stearns [*see*]). These are larger but otherwise characteristic of student travel sketches made by late nineteenth-century Americans during periods of European study. They contain the raw data of eclectic composition.

J. Williams Beal (1855–1919)

John Williams Beal was born in Norwell, Massachusetts, and entered M.I.T. from Hanover, Massachusetts, at age 18. He was awarded the B.S. in architecture in 1877 with a thesis on a "Steam Fire-Engine House" (now in the M.I.T. Museum), then worked in New York for R.M. Hunt and Mc-Kim, Mead and Bigelow until 1879. After a European sojourn he practiced as a draftsman and architect in Hanover. By 1887 he was in Boston, eventually forming the firm of J. Williams Beal and Sons.

REFERENCES: Henry F. Withey and Elsie Rathburn Withey, *Biographical Dictionary of American Architects*, Los Angeles, 1956, 44–45 ; John A. Chewning, "William Robert Ware and the Beginning of Architectural Education in the United States, 1861–1881," Ph.D. diss., M.I.T., 1986.

69. UNIDENTIFIED TOWN-
HOUSE, ca. 1900.

Front elevation of a townhouse, undated. Signed lower right: "J. Williams Beal Arch. & Del." Graphite,
watercolor, and gouache on heavy
cream paper, 19¾ × 11⅛". Prints and
Photographs Division, Library of
Congress.

A project for a characteristic urban
residence of the turn of the century,
this sheet clearly shows Beal's connection with Hunt, whose own renderings resemble but surpass this
watercolor.

69

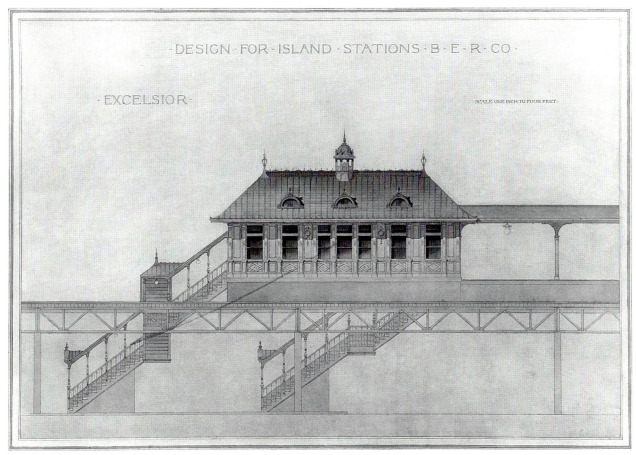

70a (see also plate 14)

Alexander W. Longfellow, Jr. (1854–1934)

Alexander Wadsworth Longfellow, Jr., nephew of the poet, was born in Portland, Maine, and attended Harvard, M.I.T., and the Ecole des Beaux-Arts in Paris, 1879 to 1881. He began his career in the atelier of H.H. Richardson (*see*), and he later organized the firm of Longfellow, Alden & Harlow. When it won the competition for the design of the Carnegie Library in Pittsburgh, 1892, Alden and Harlow moved there, while Longfellow remained in Boston to practice alone.

REFERENCE: Margaret Henderson Floyd, *Longfellow, Alden & Harlow: Architecture after Richardson*, Boston, 1989.

70. STATIONS FOR THE BOSTON ELEVATED RAILWAY COMPANY, 1897–1901 (destroyed).

70a. Side elevation of a "Design for Island Stations B.E.R. Co.," undated. Signed: "Excelsior." Ink, watercolor, and gold leaf on heavy paper, 20 × 28". Paul White.

70b. End elevation and section through tracks of a "Design for Island Stations B.E.R. Co.," undated. Signed: "Excelsior." Ink, watercolor, and gold leaf on heavy paper, 20 × 28". Paul White.

70c. Details of elevation, stairs, and shed for a "Design for Island Stations

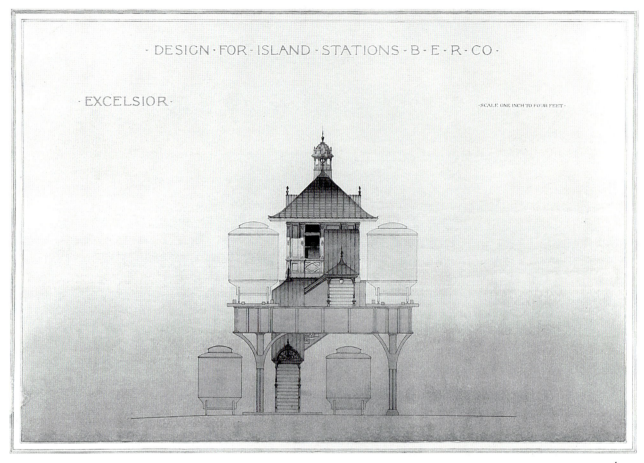

· DESIGN · FOR · ISLAND · STATIONS · B · E · R · CO ·

· EXCELSIOR ·

· SCALE ONE INCH TO FOUR FEET ·

70b

B.E.R. Co.," undated. Signed "Excelsior." Ink, watercolor, and gold leaf on heavy paper, 20 × 28". Paul White.

Longfellow, under the nom de guerre, "Excelsior," in March 1898 won a competition among ten other entries sponsored by the Boston Elevated Railway Company for the design of stations, to cost no more than $10,000, along its "Mail Line El," running from Sullivan Square to For-

est Hills. William Robert Ware, then of Columbia University, was the judge. According to *The Boston Journal*, "The early French Renaissance style is adopted in order that the pilasters and ornamentation may prevent large, monotonous surfaces of metal, and may give better light and shade effects." The line opened in June 1901.

These are the 1897 competition graphics that won Longfellow the commission to build some five sta-

tions along the route of what is now Boston's Orange Line. How could any judge resist the lushness of these presentation drawings? The sheen of metallic architecture is projected in the richness of gold leaf.

REFERENCES: *The Boston Journal*, 8 March 1898; H. McKelden Smith III, "The 'El': Boston's Elevated Railway Stations," in Pauline Chase Harrell and Margaret Supplee Smith, *Victorian Boston Today*, Boston, 1975,

70c

132–139; Cynthia Zaitzevsky, "Boston Elevated Railway Company," Historic American Engineering Record, 1988.

Julius A. Schweinfurth (1858–1931)

Julius Adolphe Schweinfurth was the middle brother of three architect brothers who were the offspring of a German immigrant engineer. Born in Auburn, New York, he joined the office of Peabody and Stearns (*see*) in Boston in 1880. After a brief partnership with his brother, Charles, in Cleveland, 1883 to 1884, Schweinfurth accompanied another Peabody and Stearns draftsman, Frank E. Wallis, on a European sojourn. For nine months in 1885 to 1886, he toured "part of Spain, Italy, France, and the So[uth] Kensington Museum" (the Victoria and Albert in London), as he lists his itinerary on the title page of *Sketches Abroad*, a portfolio of travel drawings he published in 250 copies two years later. After his return he re-entered the Peabody office, rising to chief designer before setting out on his own in 1895. Thereafter he gradually built up a large, national practice, working in the full range of revived styles available before and after the turn of the century.

The primary collection of Schweinfurth's graphic remains belongs to Northeastern University. Scattered drawings are housed in other collections.

REFERENCES: Julius A. Schweinfurth, *Sketches Abroad*, [Boston], 1888; Stephen J. Neitz with Wheaton Holden, *Julius A. Schweinfurth, Master Designer*, Boston, 1975.

71. BOSTON ATHENAEUM, 1902 (unbuilt competition entry).

"Elevation in Arlington Street," and "Elevation in Newbury Street,"

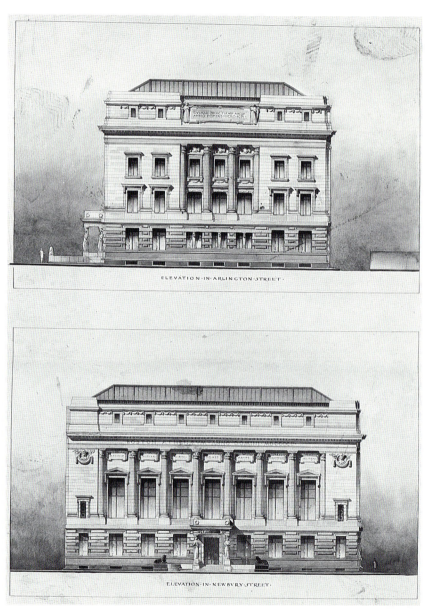

ELEVATION·IN·ARLINGTON·STREET·

ELEVATION·IN·NEWBVRY·STREET·

71

DORMITORIES·WELLESLEY·COLLEGE·

72 (see also plate 15)

for a building labeled "Boston Athenaeum" on the Arlington street elevation, dated 1902 in Roman numerals on the same elevation. Signed: "J.A. Schweinfurth Archt." Graphite and watercolors on heavy paper, 38 × 24¾". Northeastern University.

By 1901 the mid-century Palladian library designed for the Athenaeum on Beacon Street by E.C. Cabot, despite alterations in the intervening years, was straining at the seams and described as "almost a tinder box." In May the proprietors voted to sell the building and erect a new structure at Arlington and Newbury streets in the Back Bay. W.E. Putnam and A.H.

Cox won the commission for the new library in February 1902, but it was never erected. Sentiment arose against abandoning the traditional site, the old library was renovated, and the Arlington Street property sold in 1906.

Like other entries in the competition, Schweinfurth's design is cast in the Beaux-Arts classical mode and his drawings follow Beaux-Arts orthographic dictates.

REFERENCES: Neitz and Holden, 12 and fig. 30; Boston Athenaeum, *Change and Continuity. A Pictorial History of the Boston Athenaeum*, Boston, 1976, 9–10.

72. DORMITORY QUADRANGLE, WELLESLEY COLLEGE, 1903–1909.

Bird's-eye perspective from the north of "Dormitories [for] Wellesley College," "Sept 1903." Signed (later): "J.A. Schweinfurth Archt." Graphite and watercolors on trace (mounted on board), 20¼ × 34". Northeastern University.

Wellesley's residential quadrangle, erected during the presidency of Caroline Hazard (1899–1910), includes four dormitories (Beebe, Cazenove, Pomeroy, and Shafer halls). The impetus for their construction was the gift of Martha Pomeroy, whose will requested the college to erect a dormitory "in the Elizabethan Gothic style of architecture," and thus established the look of the entire complex.

The Executive Committee of the College trustees instituted a "limited competition between Messrs. Coolidge & Carlson, Mr. A.W. Longfellow [*see*] and Mr J.A. Schweinfurth for the selection of [the] Architect for two new dormitories," according to the "Programme of Competition" drafted by professional advisor Henry C. Holt of the firm of Wales & Holt of Boston (who also occasionally taught architectural history at the College). The "conditions of the site and the relation of the two proposed buildings (those nearest the street)" were to conform to the campus development plan created by Olmsted Brothers in 1902. Although this plan is now unlocated, it must have envisioned the eventual placement of four dormitories around a quadrangle, as the last quotation implies and as shown on Schweinfurth's competition drawing. The program lays out the components of the problem in great detail. It also clearly prescribes the desired style: "The design shall be an adaption to American conditions of materials, climate and convenience, of the historical style technically known as Elizabethan, [for] the definition of which [the contestant] is referred to [Reginald] Blomfield's 'History of Renaissance Architecture in England'" (1897).

The programme is also very explicit about the drawings to be submitted, "with no mark of identification," no later than noon on 1 September 1903. They were to consist of a floor plan of each story, one elevation toward the railroad (north) and one toward the courtyard, all at ⅛" scale and in pencil on white paper mounted on board, with the walls in plan shown in red, plus a bird's-eye perspective "of both buildings and their suggested future connecting links . . . taken from the R.R. side." The latter might "have light indications of color and shadows, without accessories." When the contestants in late July joined to question Holt about these accessories ("Can we indicate roads, paths, trees, grass and sky?"), they were told that "this . . . is both necessary and desirable in a drawing of this character, provided it is not overdone. Any palpable abuse . . . of this privilege would inevitably be prejudicial to its author." Each of the architects received $250 for his effort.

Schweinfurth won the competition and had this drawing photographically reproduced, presenting a signed copy of it to A.H. Hardy, the College treasurer, on 19 November 1903 (copy in Wellesley Archives). Construction began immediately. As work neared completion on the entire quadrangle, in July 1909 the architect inscribed and gave to the College through President Hazard copy number 42 of his *Sketches Abroad*. (In 1919 Schweinfurth added the connecting wing that now replaced the gate and fence shown in this drawing at the north end of the quadrangle.)

This is one of two similar renderings of the quadrangle in the collection at Northeastern. The smaller is signed by David A. Gregg, a gifted renderer who taught at M.I.T. from 1881 and whose work appears in the *AABN* for three decades beginning in the 1870s. He was the chief draftsman in the office established by William Rotch Ware, editor of the *AABN*, to do renderings for architects across the country. This drawing, too, although apparently unsigned, is clearly his work. The pale coloration may stem from the competition stipulation that the perspectives "have light indications of color," although in 1886 the *AABN* made "delicate color" one of the characteristics of Boston architectural graphics in general.

REFERENCES: Documents relating to the residential quadrangle are in Wellesley College Archives; additional drawings are in the Massachusetts State Archives; *AABN*, XIX, 13 March 1886, 124; Eileen Michels, "Late Nineteenth-Century Published American Perspective Drawings," *JSAH*, XXXI, December 1972, 296, 298, 301, 304; Glasscock, *Wellesley College*, 285, 307–308; Neitz and Holden, 16–17.

73. FIRE STATION, BROOKLINE, MASSACHUSETTS, ca. 1906 (unbuilt competition entry).

"Elevation in Walnut Street" and "East Elevation," undated. Unsigned. Graphite, ink, and watercolors on heavy paper, 16⅝" × 25" (sight); with "Alternative Treatment / [of left side of] East Elevation" on flap, 15 × 5¼" (irregular). Northeastern University.

This project remains to be fully explained. It does not appear on the Neitz and Holden list of works (none is listed for 1906), and the town records relating to the design and erection of the Washington Street fire station were apparently discarded in the 1960s. That this is for that station is suggested by the site on Walnut

ALTERNATIVE TREATMENT
- EAST ELEVATION -

ELEVATION IN WALNVT STREET

EAST ELEVATION

73

Street, which joins Washington at the location of the present station, erected from designs of Freeman, Funk and Wilcox from 1906 to 1908. Although the present building is smaller than the one shown on these drawings, it is similar in style and silhouette, a fact suggesting either an influence from Schweinfurth on the present building, or parallel interpretations of a closely defined program for the competition.

The lanky bell and clock tower of Lombard Romanesque inspiration dominates Schweinfurth's brick de-

sign. The use of a flap for alternate design ideas is not uncommon (*see* Cat. 23).

Bertram Grosvenor Goodhue (1869–1924)

Goodhue, born in Pomfret, Connecticut, in 1869, was from his early years a student of design in many of its phases, and as an adult he embellished books as well as drafted buildings. He began his apprenticeship at the age of 15 in the New York office of Renwick, Aspinwall & Russell. At the age of 22 he won the competition for the Cathedral of St. Matthew in Dallas, and, recognizing his lack of experience, joined the Boston firm of Cram and Wentworth (see). Goodhue was a facile draftsman and accomplished designer.

There is a large collection of Goodhue graphics at the M.I.T. Museum, and another collection with his descendants.

REFERENCES: Charles H. Whitaker, ed., *Bertram Grosvenor Goodhue, Architect and Master of Many Arts*, New York, 1925; Richard Oliver, *Bertram Grosvenor Goodhue*, Cambridge MA and London, 1983; James F. O'Gorman, "'Either in Books or [in] Architecture': Bertram Grosvenor Goodhue in the Ninties," *Harvard Library Bulletin*, XXXV, Spring 1987, 165–183. *See* R.A. Cram and Partners.

74. SKETCHBOOK, undated (1902?).

"Page of Small Sketches from Sketch Book" (in ink by later hand), undated. Initialed: "BGG." On verso: plan of a large complex plus "ornament in Tympanum. . . ." Light graphite on paper, 6¾ × 9⅜″. The M.I.T. Museum.

In 1902, J.W. Gillespie, one of Goodhue's clients, took him on a tour of what was then Persia. They rode horseback from the Caspian Sea to the Persian Gulf looking at architecture and gardens in Isfahan, Shiraz, Samarkand, and Persepolis.

This is a page of travel sketches presumably from this journey showing heads (one labeled "Russell Sullivan as an Emer") and details of Islamic architecture. There is a lively pencil touch, and Goodhue, who was as gifted embellishing books as detailing cathedrals, was capable of capturing the look of a mosque and its ambience in a study as small as 1½ × ¾″. These are the graphite tracks of an eager, inquisitive student of architecture in all its forms.

Ralph Adams Cram (1863–1942), and Partners

Cram was born in Hampton Falls, New Hampshire, and began his career in the 1880s with Rotch and Tilden (see). In 1887 he formed a partnership with Charles F. Wentworth (1861–1897), taking B.G. Goodhue (see) into the office in 1891 and raising him to partnership in 1892. Cram, Wentworth and Goodhue practiced until 1897 when, on the death of Wentworth, Frank W. Ferguson (1861–1926) was made a partner. Cram, Goodhue and Ferguson split into two offices in 1903, when Goodhue left to head up the New York branch. In 1914 Goodhue went on his own, and Cram and Ferguson carried on.

Both Cram and Goodhue were talented designers, although Goodhue enjoys the reputation as the more gifted artist. They laid the groundwork of their fame with the design of All Saints, Ashmont, in 1891. Thereafter Cram became a champion of the medieval revival, as exemplified in his many publications and the Cathedral of St. John the Divine in New York, which the firm took over from the original architects, although the office turned out distinguished work in the classical styles as well. Goodhue gradually drifted off in his own stylistic direction.

There is a large collection of drawings by Cram's firm in the Boston Public Library, and smaller collections in numerous other repositories, including the Avery Library, Columbia University.

REFERENCES: Montgomery Schuyler, "The Works of Cram, Goodhue and Ferguson," *Architectural Record*, 29, 1911; *The Works of Cram and Ferguson, Architects, Including Work by Cram, Goodhue and Ferguson*, New York, 1929; R.A. Cram, *My Life in Architecture*, Boston, 1936; Boston Public Library, "A Survey of Boston Architectural Drawings and Photographs," Boston, 1974; Douglass Shand Tucci, *Ralph Adams Cram, American Medievalist*, Boston, 1975.

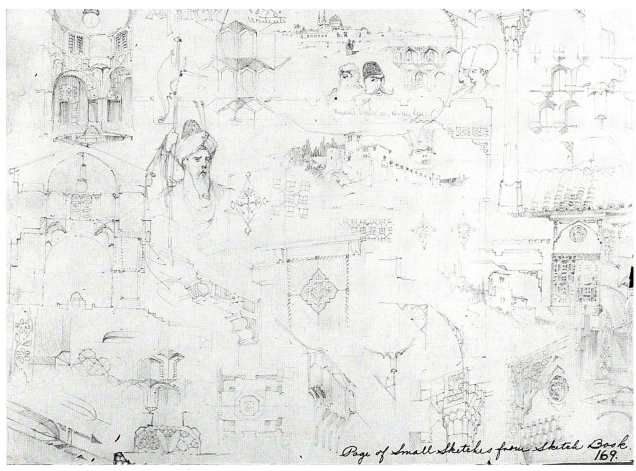

Page of Small Sketches from Sketch Book. 169.

74

75. FIRST CONGREGATIONAL CHURCH, PLYMOUTH, MASSACHUSETTS, 1893–1894.

"Pen & Ink Perspective Sketch for The First Church, Plymouth, Sch. 3." (in ink by later hand), "1893." Signed: "Bertram G. Goodhue Del." Black ink on buff board, $16\frac{7}{8} \times 12\frac{5}{8}''$. The M.I.T. Museum.

This church, nominally the work of Cram, Wentworth and Goodhue, followed the type established at All Saints, Ashmont (1891), in being "linear in plan and massing with a west tower" (Oliver). The pen-and-ink perspective presentation, with the tower shaded from light to dark as it rises against the blank sky, is characteristic of Goodhue's drawing during the 1890s and clearly intended for black-and-white reproduction.

76. FELLNER HOUSE, CHESTNUT HILL, MASSACHUSETTS, undated.

Exterior perspective, undated. Unsigned ("Fellner House—Chestnut Hill, Mass. / Cram & Wentworth—Architects / Design and Rendering by R.A. Cram": penciled title on mat). Graphite and watercolor on heavy paper (glued to mat), $7\frac{3}{16} \times 13\frac{1}{8}''$. Avery Architectural and Fine Arts Library, Columbia University in the City of New York.

This is a presentation drawing of a brick and shingle Tudor suburban house with square tower, half timbering, high gables, large, multi-paned windows, and tall chimneys separated into individual, canted flues, set on a hillside site. The close viewpoint forces the building into a dramatic *da sotto in su* perspective more character-

75

76

istic of Cram's partner, B.G. Goodhue. If the attributions of this and the
drawing in Cat. 77 are correct, Cram
was a more accomplished artist than
he has been credited. The handling of
watercolor displays an impressionist's
touch, and may stem from Cram's
stay in the office of Rotch and Tilden
(*see*).

77 (see also plate 16)

77. BEACON STREET TOWN-HOUSES, BOSTON, 1896 or 1898.

Elevation, undated ("1896" on mat and "1898" on verso). Signed: "Cram and Wentworth / Architects, 2 Park Sq." (in pencil on mat: "Project for Houses in Boston / Design and Rendering by R.A. Cram about 1896"). Graphite and watercolor on heavy paper, 10¼ × 19¼″. Avery Architectural and Fine Arts Library, Columbia University in the City of New York.

According to a note on the verso, this row of six brick and limestone (?) classical townhouses was "not built." The tradition of classical townhouses established by Bulfinch here carries to the end of the century, although architectural change during the period between Bulfinch and Cram is suggested by the fact that, as Douglass Tucci observes, "these would look better on the Grand Canal than Beacon St."

REFERENCE: Douglass Shand Tucci to author, 8 April 1988.

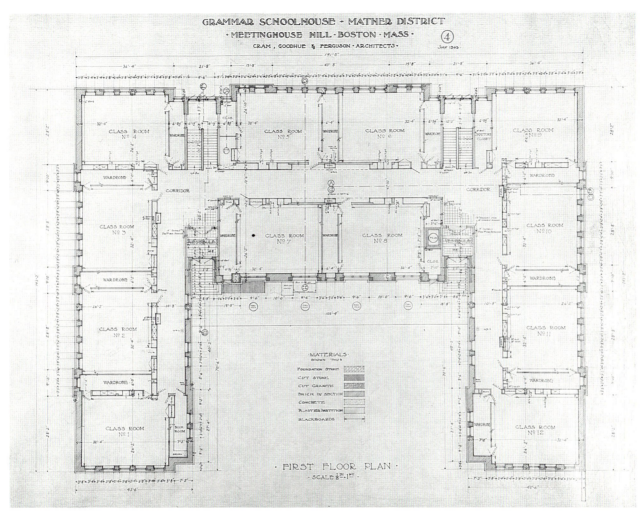

78a

78. MATHER DISTRICT GRAM-
MAR SCHOOLHOUSE, MEET-
INGHOUSE HILL, BOSTON, 1903.

78a. "First Floor Plan" of "Grammar Schoolhouse, Mather District /
Meetinghouse Hill, Boston, Mass.,"
"July 1903." Signed: "Cram, Goodhue & Ferguson, Architects." Sheet
"4." Black and red inks and yellow

wash on linen, 24⅝ × 36½". Avery
Architectural and Fine Arts Library,
Columbia University in the City of
New York.

78b. "Front Elevation," of "Grammar Schoolhouse . . . ," "July 1903."
"Cram, Goodhue & Ferguson, Architects." Sheet "8." Black and red inks
on linen, 24⅝ × 36½". Avery Architectural and Fine Arts Library, Co-

lumbia University in the City of New
York.

78c. "Detail[s] of Entrance," of
"Grammar Schoolhouse . . . ," undated. "Cram, Goodhue & Ferguson,
Architects." Sheet "21." Black and
red inks and green wash with graphite
note, 36½ × 24⅝". Avery Architectural and Fine Arts Library, Columbia
University in the City of New York.

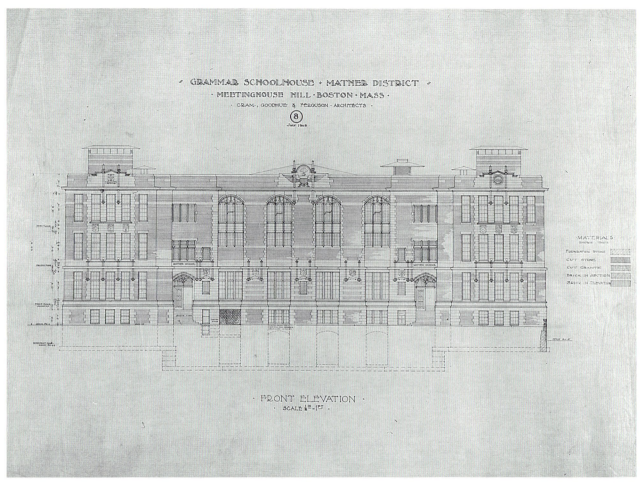

78b

With these sheets, selected from a much larger set, working drawings assume their twentieth-century look. Largely black line orthographics by anonymous draftsman or -men, prepared on transparent stock with an eye toward the blueprinting machine, these are examples of an ever larger number of drawings accompanying specifications which form the basis for the modern construction contract.

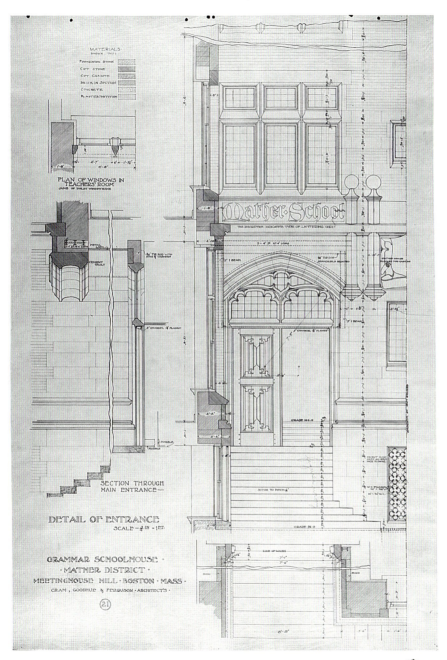

MATERIALS·
SHOWN THUS·

FOUNDATION STONE
CUT STONE
CUT GRANITE
BRICK IN SECTION
CONCRETE
PLASTER PARTITION

PLAN OF WINDOWS IN
TEACHERS' ROOM
JAMB OF THREE WINDOW SAME

Mather School

SECTION THROUGH
MAIN ENTRANCE·

DETAIL OF ENTRANCE
SCALE ¾ IN =1 FT·

GRAMMAR SCHOOLHOUSE·
·MATHER DISTRICT·
MEETINGHOUSE HILL·BOSTON·MASS·
CRAM , GOODHUE & FERGUSON ·ARCHITECTS·

㉑

Index of Artists, Architects, and Buildings